Home Cooked Hamptons

Home
Cooked
Hamptons

An insider's signature and classic recipes throughout the
seasons on the East End of Long Island.

Utilizing the abundant resources from local farms, land,
and sea and inspired by cultures of the world.

Bonnie Abdelnour Verbitsky

Patrice Samara - Editor
Christina Holmes - Photographer
Krisa Verbitsky - Designer

Quality Cuisine
Media

Edited by Patrice Samara
Photography by Christina Holmes
Jacket and book design by Krisa Verbitsky
Additional photography: Patrice Samara, Lauren Torrisi,
    Bonnie Abdelnour Verbitsky, and Kristin Verbitsky

Production services provided by Quartet Books
www.quartetbooks.com

Published by Quality Cuisine Media, LLC.
P.O. Box 3017
Bridgehampton, New York 11932

info@HomeCookedHamptons.com
www.HomeCookedHamptons.com

Library of Congress Control Number: 2012911299
ISBN 978-0-9857830-0-6

10 9 8 7 6 5 4 3 2

Printed on acid-free paper in the United States

Dedicated to my sister, Beverly,
who was stricken with A.L.S.
and also shared my love of
entertaining for family and friends.

Table of Contents

Quality ingredients and a passion for food are the keys to all great meals.

Bonnie Abdelnour Verbitsky

Acknowledgments

The author wishes to extend grateful thanks to:

The late James Brady, for his encouragement, inspiration, and divine guidance. I am confident he is looking down on me from a better place.

Giuliano Bugialli, for his stimulating teaching style.

Sylvia Lehrer, for her love of food and many informative cooking classes.

Daniel Boulud, for his inspiration.

Stephane Caporal, executive chef at Fisher Island Restaurants, Fisher Island, Florida, for sharing his recipes, ideas, and mutual love of cooking.

Kari and the late Dick Clark, for their friendship and the many meals we have shared. Kari generously shared her recipes. I will always cherish her handwritten notes.

Leila Gorra, for being like a sister and sharing her culinary knowledge.

Sue Elias, for sharing her recipe that was handed down from Rose Awad, our close family friend.

Nancy Bailey, for offering tips from our heritage and guidance in Lebanese dishes.

Betty Franey and the late Pierre Franey. Betty graciously shared one of Pierre's most coveted recipes.

Joan Hamburg, radio personality at WOR, 710 AM in New York since the early 1970s, for helping me to go to the next level and for her amazing positive energy, support, and friendship. Always enthusiastic, she shares a passion for cooking for friends and family.

Beth Harris, with John Haessler, for publishing my first recipe in June 1990 in the *Wainscott Seafood Shop Cookbook* by Random House.

Christina Holmes, for her tireless energy and finesse as a photographer and using her expertise gained while shooting for some of the the country's most prestigious publications: *Food & Wine, Bon Appétit, Martha Stewart's Whole Living Magazine;* and the *Cooking Channel.*

Aphrodite and Gus Laggis, for sharing recipes that transport us to Greece and for making eating at The Candy Kitchen a genuine East End tradition.

Fernando and Gino Masci, master chefs and owners of Il Gabbiano, Miami, and founders of Il Mulino Restaurant in New York City, for making their restaurants our home away from home and sharing with me the key to their wonderful food and fine ingredients.

Colin Mather, for sharing his encyclopedic knowledge about the local fishing industry and local seafood.

Patrice Samara, Emmy Award–winning producer and strategic advisor, for her professionalism and flawless talent. We share our heritage and a love of entertaining. Summering in the Pocono Mountains connected our lives forever. Importantly, she was a close friend of my sister, Beverly, to whom this book is dedicated.

Pat Harrington and Caryl Duffy, for their warm encouragement and undying support.

Adrienne Vittadini, renowned for her fashion and design empire, which has spanned several decades, for sharing one of her many fabulous recipes along with the love of entertaining at home.

To the chefs who inspired me:

Left to right: Jarrod Verbiak, executive chef (DB Bistro); Stephane Caporal, executive chef (Fisher Island Club, Fisher Island, FL); Bonnie Verbitsky; Daniel Boulud; and DB Bistro chefs. Thank you for preparing a special-event dinner, sharing your fine cuisine, and inviting me into your kitchen.

Kevin Penner, executive chef (1770 House, CittaNuova, East Hampton).
Thank you for your love of fine cuisine and bringing me into your kitchen.

Philippe Chow, Bonnie Verbitsky, Costin Dumitrescu of Philippe Restaurant Group, and Stephane Caporal, for motivating me to explore the preparation of Chinese-influenced cuisine.

Acknowledgments (continued)

Donna and Allan Stillman, well-known restaurateurs and founders of Smith and Wollensky Restaurants and the Park Avenue Cafe, for sharing the love of good food, great home dinners together, and offering one of their favorite Austrian desserts.

Rev. Dr. Robert Stephanopoulos, for his spiritual guidance over the years and for offering me tips on one of his favorite desserts following a Greek dinner.

Lauren Torrisi, of ABC News and a talented pastry chef, for sharing two at-home dessert recipes.

Kevin Penner, for teaching me many special cooking techniques and sharing his recipe.

All those who have shared their special recipes and helped make this cookbook a reality: Fernando Masci, Pasquale Pagnotta, Jesus Benitez, Noelle Fazio, and Susan Santefort.

My dear friends Dr. Jane Galasso and the late Ralph Galasso, who have inspired me by giving special tips and sharing many innovative meals over the years.

The friends who are so important in my life and who have offered encouragement: Nancy Gorra, Lorraine Samara Valdivia, Addie Guttag, Nevitt Jenkins, Pat McLaughlin, Carol Crapple, Sandy Taylor, Toni Vreeland, Sacha McNaughton, Linda Fraser, Ches Stevenson, Debbie Romaine, Barbara Zweig, Peggy Smith, Marguerite Davis, Alice Lord, Sunny Neff, Helen Horowitz, Jill Columbo, Barbara Higgins, and Rose Bertagni.

Laurie Augenstein, who, when growing up together, was like a younger sister to me. She emanates a positive attitude toward life that touches everyone she knows.

My family: our sons and daughters-in-law, for their love, support, and healthy appetites. I always strive to make our each and every meal together an occasion for celebration. My brother Bill Abdelnour and his daughters, Danielle and Janeen; my niece Lisa Pinney Keusch; my sisters-in-law Mary Ellen Abdelnour and Christine Wetzler; and my cousin Mary DeGarmo.

Mary Wang, for her encouragement and support through the years and for sharing her Chinese recipes.

Krisa Verbitsky, for her graphic artistry and design skills that supported my ambition to finish this book. Her unwavering enthusiasm and loving support helped interpret and make my vision a reality.

My dear Uncle Jerry Haddad, for his technical genius, longevity, enthusiasm for life, and sharing family traditions and recipes from our heritage.

Aunt Rae, for showing us how to appreciate the joy of life and for all her love and guidance through the years.

Kristin, my lovely daughter, whose invaluable assistance with photography, recipes, and tastings continually motivated me. To my delight, she has evolved into a great cook herself and a passionate, talented writer for film, theater, and entertainment news. Her warmth and creativity are an inspiration. When she came into this world, she made all my dreams come true.

My darling husband, Nick, who has wholeheartedly supported my efforts by tasting myriad recipes for this book and has always been enthusiastic about my style of entertaining. His special menu requests have inspired me to be creative while sharing the fruits of my efforts with friends and family. He truly is the light and love of my life.

My mother and father, for their passion for life, food, and entertaining. You set a high standard and encouraged me to pass down our culture from one generation to the next. Your example will always be a touchstone. You made me the woman I am today.

Introduction

Home Cooked Hamptons is about the great pleasure I derive from cooking for family and friends. Many people in the Hamptons, also known as the East End of Long Island, share this enjoyment of entertaining and home cooking. It is the art of seasonal cooking, taking the freshest produce from the fertile land, daily catches from the sea, and quality meats from the local butchers, then turning them into culinary masterpieces.

Entertaining and lifestyle are the main themes here, while I endeavor to bring all the natural elements of the Hamptons to the table . . . from farmland to ocean. Relaxed formality is shared by many of us who take great pride in our homes and gardens. To me, there is nothing more satisfying than cooking for friends who share my passion for food and wine.

While many of the tabloids, the Internet, or blogs have defined the Hamptons as a haven for fast-paced celebrities and extravagant parties, *Home Cooked Hamptons* truly represents the classic Hamptons that I know in home entertaining for family and friends. In addition to my tried and true personal menus and recipes, I have included recipes from professional chefs and friends who have offered to share their secret favorites.

There are many reasons the residents of the Hamptons prefer to cook in the privacy of their own homes. Primarily city dwellers, their mid-week lifestyle consists of eating on the run, take-out meals, and eating in restaurants. As they begin their drive eastward out of the city, they begin to relax. As they get closer to the East End, they begin to experience a zen-like calm. There is a unique quality to the light in the Hamptons that has inspired artists since the nineteenth century. At a certain point, Montauk Highway borders the Atlantic Ocean; savoring the clean fresh air cleanses the soul and helps shed the stresses of the city. The natural beauty of this fertile land surrounded by large bodies of bay waters and the Atlantic Ocean adds to the relaxed way of life that serves as a catalyst for the Hamptons-style of entertaining.

My earliest experiences in the Hamptons began in the 1970s. As a college student, spending my first summer in a Quogue beach shack was the precursor to all the wonderful offerings this extraordinary region has to give. Forever imbedded in my memory was my first drive on Dune Road in Westhampton Beach. Traveling east toward Hampton Bays (near the Shinnecock Inlet) with vast stretches of sea grass lining the bay on the left side of the road and the roaring ocean on the right, I have a sense memory of the smell of the salt air, and it propelled me into a natural state of euphoria! Proceeding farther east, past the white, sandy beaches to the marina in Hampton Bays, the seagulls filled the sky and hovered in their favorite spot over fishing boats returning with their day's catch. The Deck and nearby Oakland's Restaurant and Marina were popular watering holes we frequented after basking on the beach. There was nothing more exhilarating than having an ice-cold glass of white wine with clams freshly shucked in front of my eyes, as I watched the fishermen unload delicacies from the sea.

As the years went by, I found myself going less and less to places like The Deck to eat out and spending more time mentally preparing the recipe for that night's dinner I was about to cook at home. I began to long to prepare the cornucopia of fresh local foods myself. These initial Hampton experiences fostered my deep appreciation for fresh food from the fertile land and abundant surrounding waters, as well as admiration of the local purveyors and fishermen who had dedicated their lives to perpetuating the traditions of their forefathers.

Moving farther east to live in Bridgehampton, I became enthralled with the vast tracks of farmland, as much as I had been captivated by the sea. Open fields, orchards, and vineyards stretching for miles into the horizon were unlike any place I had ever been before. The variety of textures against the bright cerulean sky created a unique picture. I would observe the local farmers proudly displaying enormous varieties of produce at their roadside stands right after they were picked. Their pride and the hard work that was involved in producing such a plentiful array of fruits and vegetables was palpable.

❖

Year after year, as the seasons came and went, the continuum of the farmers' pattern of plantings blanketed the Hamptons like patchwork.

The first evidence of the yearly bounty begins in late May with asparagus and rhubarb. As summer nears, handmade signs saying pick-your-own strawberries are seen at many of the roadside farm stands. Strawberry picking is an annual ritual shared by many families. My daughter and I have been picking since she was three. Now a young woman, she prefers buying the strawberries at the farm stands, but I shall never tire of picking them myself!

July brings huge red raspberries, artichokes, and melons. Summer fields planted with arugula, unlimited varieties of verdant lettuce, zucchini, spinach, beans, broccoli, and onions are complemented by Long Island's prized crops of sweet red and yellow tomatoes, corn, and potatoes.

Acres of orchards of all kinds bear their fruit toward the end of summer. The peaches begin to ripen on the trees by mid-August. Weekend apple picking from the abundant orchards marks the end of summer. For those who do not like apple picking, there are loads of farm stands with overflowing bins with a wide variety of apples such as Macoun, Fuji, and Empire, plus the more well-known Macintosh and Granny Smith. Many farmers also market their homemade apple cider.

The Milk Pail in Water Mill, one of the largest apple orchards in the area, adds a special treat to their farm stand with a vat of fresh, made-to-order donuts with packets of powdered sugar. This sweet, irresistible temptation is hard to refuse, especially when consumed with their freshly pressed apple cider!

The large round pumpkins turn the roads into an orange oasis, making way for the farmer's final harvest. And let's not forget the poultry farms that raise hand-fed chickens and ducks at North Sea Farms, Southampton, and Iocono's in East Hampton. It is truly an experience going to these farms for poultry and farm-fresh eggs.

Thanksgiving always comes upon us faster than we anticipate . . . and the turkey farmers at Ludlow's and

North Sea Farms make sure they have enough turkeys for their loyal customers.

The Ludlow Family was among the original settlers who arrived in the Hamptons in the mid-1600s from Lynn, Massachusetts. Ludlow's has been a potato farm since the 1880s. Today, Art Ludlow has become a successful dairy farmer. Art keeps his family tradition alive by raising turkeys on his farm and only sells them at Thanksgiving. They request early orders to make sure there are enough turkeys for the holiday. Of course, fresh, farm-raised turkeys are always the best, and I have never tasted a better turkey.

As we all know, Thanksgiving is the celebration of the final harvest after the labor-intensive farming of summer and autumn. Art's brother, Harry, keeps his farm hut open until Thanksgiving, selling fresh vegetables, homemade pies, and Art's famous Mecox Sunrise Cheese, along with other flavorful cheeses

he produces. I have fond memories of Art asking me to try his new cheeses in his kitchen.

Several years ago, I stopped by Art's to pick up my turkey and he asked me to taste a few of his cheeses. I was so impressed with the quality of his cheeses, I put in one of his first orders and continue enjoying his artisan cheeses to this day. Art went on to win an American Cheese Society Competition Award in Wisconsin for the Mecox Sunrise Cheese. Currently, his cheeses are sold at fine markets on the East End.

The eastern end of Long Island was and still is renowned for its potato farms. During the 1600s, New Englanders settled there and started what is known as subsistence farming, living off the produce from their farms, self-sufficiently feeding their families. Any leftover produce that the family did

not eat, would be sold. The potatoes became a favorite. Potato farms flourished in this area because of the climate and the ideal, low-pH level, rich soil. Specialized farming began. Transportation to larger markets was easily accessible from the eastern tip of Long Island, making the Hamptons' potatoes renowned for their abundance and flavor. Today, there are still several major farms run by families dating back to the early settlers with the surnames of White, Halsey, and Foster, who still grow potatoes while expanding into other produce.

Quite often, at the end of August and the first week of September, the farmers drive their tractors on the main roads from one farm field to another, working vigorously to prepare for the harvest. I delight seeing those mounds of potatoes being carted in large trucks . . . except when I am driving behind one and in a hurry!

Recently, vineyards have flourished all over eastern Long Island. Many have tasting rooms and highly acclaimed, award-winning wines. With the delectable meals we share with guests, we now can offer local wines as well as other domestic or imported wines. Wölffer Estate Vineyard in Bridgehamp-

ton, Duck Walk Vineyards of Water Mill, and Channing Sisters in Bridgehampton offer a variety of fine wines. These vineyards have helped the Hamptons become a new region for fine wine growers.

By way of some background information, my ancestors came to America in the late 1800s from Lebanon. Preparing and sharing food, as well as entertaining, are an integral part of my heritage. One of my favorite family recipes is a Lebanese dish called *Koosa Mehshi*—zucchini stuffed with rice, lamb, tomatoes, and mint. It is simple, nutritious, and delicious.

Another special dinner I loved growing up was *Sheik'al Meshi*, stuffed eggplant boats with lamb, onions, and pine nuts covered with a touch of tomato sauce. My mother used to prepare fried eggplant slices and fried cauliflower weekly during the summer. To this day, I love fried eggplant with slices of green pepper in a pita pocket with ketchup. Of course, I now grill them with a touch of oil. Grilling is no doubt healthier, but the memory of the foods I ate as a child have made an indelible impression.

When I was growing up, no one was familiar with the now-ubiquitous pita bread and many other specialties such as *hummus*, chick pea and sesame paste; and *babaganoush*, eggplant dip. The key to a better-than-ever *babaganoush* is broiling the eggplant in the oven or cooking it on a grill, both of which impart a smoky flavor. I have to admit, at family gatherings, everyone loves my *baba!*

Throughout the years, I have been blessed to have entertained and been entertained by the celebrated and the unknown alike with the finest food the world has to offer. For example, an author, whose artistry can turn the simple technique of how to grill a steak with a distinctive flavor into poetry. A broadcaster surveying the table decor and requesting that his daughter go to their cutting garden, planted mid-spring, to pick a bunch of dahlias and roses for the table. Farmers who delight in the outdoors and savor their own crops with simple, unique recipes. Yet, the pure act of cutting fragrant flowers from my garden or visiting the nearby farms for fresh-picked produce for that night's dinner truly satisfies my soul.

Every family has a secret recipe that everyone adores. The Candy Kitchen, a coffee shop in Bridgehampton, is a traditional meeting place for breakfast and lunch. Early morning breakfast was always my favorite time at The Candy Kitchen, especially when my daughter was a small child. Gathered around the only rectangular table in the front room would be a small group of men. Among them was the late Don Hewitt, producer of *60 Minutes,* having coffee and discussing the events of the world. The Candy Kitchen is owned by Aphrodite and Gus Laggis, and for over thirty years they have been a landmark in Bridgehampton. For this cookbook, Aphrodite has shared two Greek recipes that she serves to her family on Sundays and holidays.

Over the years, I have taken many cooking classes with American, Italian, and French chefs. Some have spent their summers on the East End. Sapori di Mare restaurant in Wainscott, one of the first fine Italian restaurants to open on the East End, offered cooking classes with a different chef from Italy each summer. One of the chefs was American, Mark Strausman, the renowned restaurateur and owner of Fred's at Barneys in New York City, who held a

cooking class on Duck *Confit*. It was most informative and memorable.

Sylvia Lehrer offered cooking classes at her home for many years. I will never forget when she had Master Chef Giuliano Bugialli as a guest chef at one of her cooking classes for couples. We made a special timbale pasta, which we stretched around Sylvia's entire living room. It took forever to make this pasta, but with glasses of wine in our hands, it became one of our most memorable cooking experiences! I attribute many of my cooking techniques to these wonderful chefs.

Kevin Penner, the pioneer chef at Della Femina's restaurant in East Hampton, and currently executive chef at 1770 House and several other restaurants in East Hampton, shared his recipe with me for Fluke Provençale that my dinner guests raved about for days.

My husband was a partner in the Della Femina Restaurant in New York. We spent many a night taste-testing dishes. At that time, Kevin was the executive chef and he would often invite me into the kitchen and show me how to prepare the restaurant's specialties.

Stephane Caporal, executive chef and director at Fisher Island Restaurants, on an island off Miami, Florida, invited me to share my *Frutti di Mare* recipe with his beach club chef. Because the restaurants purchased shrimp daily, we adapted my recipe for Mixed Seafood Pasta recipe, and we decided to call it Shrimp *La Mer*. It was served for two years at the Fisher Island Beach Club.

Years ago, when I was a marketing executive at WOR Radio in New York City, I became friends with Joan Hamburg, the renowned on-air personality. She was one of the first dinner guests in my home and I made Veal Chop *Milanese*. She encouraged me to share my love of cooking and entertaining with the world. Joan and I remain good friends to this day.

Over the last twenty years, the Hamptons have experienced tremendous growth in population, which has enabled the farmers to open their own farm stands and sell directly to the public. Many of the residents, who are not farmers by profession, enjoy planting their own gardens at home. World-famous chef and food columnist for the *New York Times,* the late Pierre Franey, in a sense, was a farmer, but not like the farmers mentioned above. He created a very large vegetable garden for his culinary enjoyment at his winter home in East Hampton and at his waterfront property on Gardiners Bay. Pierre's love of fishing on the bay was one of the reasons why his wife, Betty, chose to contribute his favorite fish soup recipe to this cookbook. My cooking enjoyment and knowledge commenced with Pierre Franey's *The New York Times 60 Minute Gourmet,* written in 1985. I remember the thrill of seeing Pierre with his good friend and colleague, Craig Claiborne—the food journalist, restaurant critic, and book author, at The Seafood Shop in Wainscott, intensely discussing the catch of the day. Claiborne and Franey wrote several cookbooks together. Pierre is greatly missed, and his legend of being one of the great chefs of all time lives on.

I will always remember another of my friends, James Brady, for his marine novels and news columns in which he wrote often about the Hamptons. He proclaimed that his favorite time of year in the Hamptons was immediately after Labor Day. He and I shared the preference for autumn. For some of us, the autumn is a little piece of heaven. As the days grow shorter, there is a quiet serenity that encompasses the Hamptons. The summer crowds are gone. The beaches are once again back to their natural state and void of the beach umbrellas and chairs that dotted the waterfront in summer. Although James often attended dinners at our home, his preference was to dine with family and friends at his own home in East Hampton. His secret cooking technique on grilling steaks will surprise even the most experienced cook. James insisted that I publish a cookbook and I will always be grateful for his gentle prodding. So at James's encouragement, the result is *Home Cooked Hamptons*.

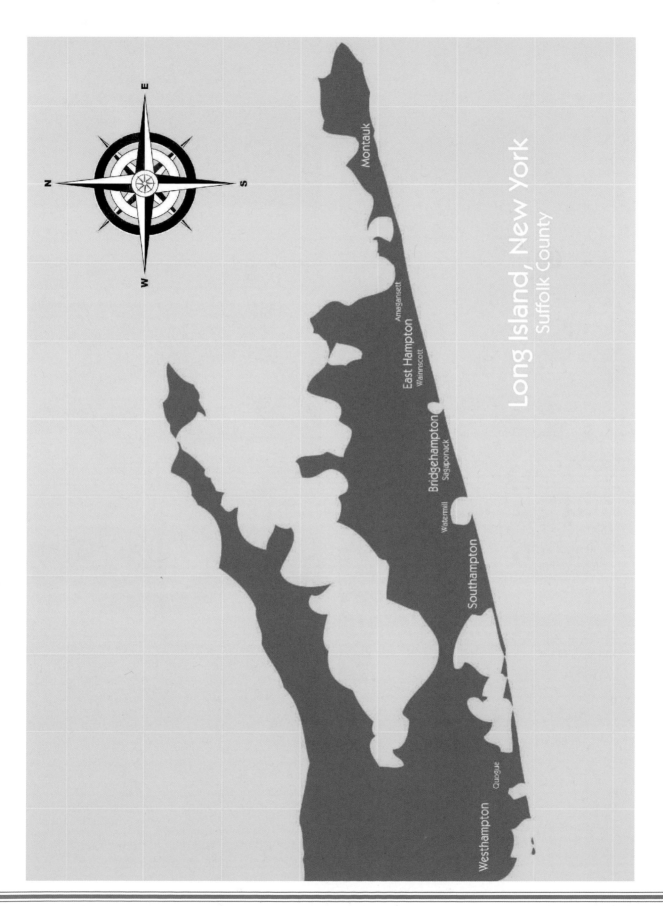

Long Island, New York
Suffolk County

Montauk

Amagansett
East Hampton
Wainscott

Bridgehampton
Sagaponack

Watermill

Southampton

Quogue

Westhampton

Summer Menus

Catch of the Day–serves 4

Spicy Baked Clams • Kevin Penner's Fluke *Provinçale* • Snap Peas and Garden Pea Medley • Cherry *Clafoutis*

July 4th Clambake–serves 8

Seafood Shop Clambake • Old-Fashioned Strawberry Shortcake

Beach Picnic–serves 4

Tomato, Peach, and Mint Salad with Champagne *Vinaigrette* • Bonnie's Classic Lobster Roll
Platter of Watermelon Wedges with Sliced Nectarines and Figs • Bonnie's Best Chocolate Chip Cookies

My Hampton Classic Dinner–serves 4

Pappardelle Portofino with *Pesto* and Tomato Sauce
Veal Chop *Milanese* with Arugula and Tomato Salad • Raspberry Tart

Grilled Veal Chop Dinner Inspired by Kari Clark–serves 4

Tomato and *Mozzarella di Bufala Napoleon* • Kari Clark's Simply Delicious Veal Chops
Grilled Asparagus • Rustic Ricotta Cheesecake

A Greek Grill Dinner–serves 8

Greek Salad with *Feta* Cheese • Grilled Butterflied Leg of Lamb • *Spanakopita* Casserole
Creamy Rice Pudding with Almonds

Festive Spanish Dinner on the Terrace–serves 6

Gazpacho de Malaga • *Paella Valenciana* • White Sangria • *Flan* with Cognac

Summer Lunch by the Pool–serves 4

Grilled Tuna Teriyaki on a Bun with Wasabi Mayo
Grilled Nectarines with Black Raspberries and Vanilla Frozen Yogurt

Hot August Night Dinner–serves 4

Prosciutto, Melon, and Mint • *Spaghettini* with Arugula and Cherry Tomatoes
Gelato with *Biscotti* and *Vin Santo* (Italian Dessert Wine)

Farm-Fresh Summer Dinner–serves 4

Adrienne Vittadini's *Penne* with Zucchini • Peachy Cream Tart

Dinner by the Creek–serves 4

Baked Brie • Beer-Can Chicken with Spice Rub
Corn on the Cob with Cayenne Butter • Grilled Zucchini and Eggplant • Blueberry Pie

Labor Day Supper–serves 6

Stuffed Zucchini Blossoms • *Percatelli* with Tuna *Caprese* • Seven Layer Ice Cream Cake

Post Labor Day Dinner–serves 4

Avocado, Artichoke, Endive Salad with Shaved Parmesan • Roasted Halibut with Fried Leeks
Mashed Potatoes with *Pancetta* • Grilled Pears with *Mascarpone*

Bonic Seafood Pasta–serves 4

Burrata and *Prosciutto* with Figs • Bonic Seafood Pasta • Orange Sorbet with *Prosecco*

Catch of the Day

serves 4

Spicy Baked Clams • Kevin Penner's Fluke Provinçale • Snap Peas and Garden Pea Medley • Cherry *Clafoutis*

Snap peas are picked daily on the East End during the summer months, and they are, oh, so sweet! They make a fine accompaniment to any meat, poultry, or fish dish.

Spicy Baked Clams

These are always a hit with family and friends. They are light and perfect for either a first course or *hor d'oeuvres*. The clams are left whole in order to taste the freshness of each clam. I make these often during the summer months when I can get them moments after they are harvested by local fishermen. Serve them with a chilled glass of white wine.

2 dozen medium-size cherrystone or large littleneck clams opened on the half shell
½ cup plain bread crumbs
1 large clove garlic pressed
¼ cup freshly grated Parmesan Cheese (preferably *Parmigiano Reggiano*)
1 tablespoon parsley, finely chopped
½ teaspoon dried oregano
Juice of one lemon (approx. 2 tablespoons)
6 tablespoons olive oil
Pinch of sea salt
⅛ teaspoon cayenne pepper or ¼ teaspoon, if you like it spicier

Preheat oven to 500 degrees.

Combine all ingredients, except the clams, and mix. Spoon mixture on each clam in the shell. Place clams in their shells on a baking pan.

Bake clams for 5 minutes until golden brown. If not golden, turn heat up and broil for 1 minute. Serve with lemon wedges.

Kevin Penner's Fluke *Provençale*

Kevin Penner has been one of the Hamptons most celebrated executive chefs for many years. He is currently executive chef at the CittaNuova Restaurant and the 1770 House in East Hampton. Kevin was chef at Della Femina's from 1992–2001 and also made frequent visits to James Beard House in New York City.

Kevin has shared one of his favorite fish recipes. I love it for its elegance and simplicity! Easy to prepare, just top it with some thinly sliced tomatoes, some thyme, and then garnish it with *Niçoise* olives. Fluke is a favorite local fish on the East End. Fluke can be substituted with cod or any other non-oily fish.

4 6-ounce portions of fluke filet with skin removed
2 ripe tomatoes, thinly sliced
4 tablespoons Ligurian olive oil or any extra virgin olive oil
16 unpitted *Niçoise* olives

2 sprigs of fresh thyme leaves or ½ teaspoon
  dried thyme
4 pinches of, preferably, Maldon sea salt (or any
  other sea salt)
1 lemon, sliced in half the short way

Preheat broiler.

Place the fluke fillets spaced about one inch apart on the broiler pan. Top each piece of fluke with tomato slices and broil for about 6–8 minutes or until a skewer easily pierces the fish.

Place each fluke portion on a plate and top with a drizzle of olive oil. Top with four olives per portion, a pinch of thyme leaves and the sea salt. Squeeze some lemon juice over each portion.

For an authentic touch, serve with rosé wine. We often have wines from East End vineyards, such as Channing Daughters Winery, Duck Walk Vineyards, and Wölffer Estate Vineyards. Additionally, any imported French rosé will complement this dish. I particularly like *Domaine Ott* from Provence.

Snap Peas and Garden Pea Medley

2 cups snap peas
¼ cup extra virgin olive oil
¼ cup chicken broth or water
¼ teaspoon salt
Pinch of black pepper
1 box fresh shelled peas or frozen garden peas
  (approximately 2 cups)

Wash snap peas and cut off any thin green stems.

Heat oil in a large sauté pan on medium heat. When pan is hot, add snap peas for 2 minutes, stirring quickly. Add chicken broth or water, salt, and pepper. If using frozen peas, add now and stir. Fresh peas take about 5 minutes to cook. If using fresh peas, steam in a separate pot for 5 minutes before adding to snap peas. Cook for another 2 minutes. Snap peas should be bright green and not overcooked. Taste for salt and pepper.

Remove from heat and serve. Can be prepared ahead of time.

Cherry *Clafoutis*

Clafoutis is a traditional, rustic fruit cake from France. This is a light dessert to make in the summer months with fresh-picked cherries, or all year long with fresh, frozen, or canned fruits. My friend Noelle Fazio prepares this dessert often for her family. It was passed down to her from her French grandmother. Here is my adaptation. I prefer to use Kirsch, a cherry brandy, in this recipe to give the custard a zing.

Cherries:

2 pounds pitted sweet, dark red cherries
¼ cup sugar

Batter:

4 eggs
¾ cup sugar
4 tablespoons butter
1½ cups milk
1 tablespoon vanilla extract
⅔ cup flour
2 tablespoons Kirsch (a cherry brandy, optional)

Preheat oven to 325 degrees.

Place cherries in a buttered oval gratin baking dish large enough to lay cherries in one layer.

In a bowl, whisk eggs and sugar with an electric mixer or a whisk until creamy and pale yellow. Melt butter in a small saucepan and add to egg and sugar mixture; then add milk, vanilla, flour, and Kirsch. Mix batter well until smooth. Let rest five minutes. Pour batter over cherries and bake for 35–40 minutes or until golden on top. *Clafoutis* is done when you insert a toothpick or sharp pointed knife in center and it comes out clean.

Sprinkle with confectioners sugar and serve with *crème fraîche*.

July 4th Clambake

serves 8

Seafood Shop Clambake • Old-Fashioned Strawberry Shortcake

The Seafood Shop in Wainscott has been one of the favorite fishmongers in the Hamptons for professional chefs, restaurateurs, and local residents for over thirty years.

In past years, it was common to see legendary epicures, the late Craig Claiborne and Pierre Franey, shopping at The Seafood Shop. Pierre Franey was not only famous for being one of America's top chefs, but also as an author, along with Craig Claiborne, for their *New York Times Cookbook*, a staple to this day.

Colin Mather, the current owner of The Seafood Shop, maintains the quality and freshness of the seafood. This classic recipe for their famous clambakes have been passed down for generations.

Seafood Shop Clambake

2 rolls cheese cloth
2 chickens cut into eighths, skin removed
Creole seasoning
Paprika
16 ears sweet corn, husked
3 dozen top neck clams
20 small new potatoes
8 large chowder clams
8 1¼-pound lobsters
1 medium baking potato
1½ pounds butter
4 lemons

Cut the cheesecloth into 12, foot-long pieces to make bags. Unfold completely, set aside. Place chicken in bowl and generously season with Creole seasoning and paprika, set aside.

Next, place items into cheesecloth to make separate bags and tie them closed:

4 bags of husked corn, 4 ears each
4 bags seasoned chicken, 2 pieces each
2 bags top neck clams, 18 clams each
2 bags new potatoes, 10 potatoes each

In the bottom of a large lobster pot, evenly spread 8 large chowder clams in 2 inches of water. In the following order, place all food in the pot: potatoes, chicken, clams, lobster, corn, and the baking potato. Cook over medium-high heat for 45–60 minutes. At this point, remove the cover and check baking potato for doneness. If the potato is fork tender, your clambake is ready.

Remove all food from pot and bags, carefully separating each variety into its own garnished platter. Melt butter and slice lemons. Arrange a colorful and festive buffet, and allow your guests to help themselves.

During certain times of the year, fish markets may be able to get rock seaweed. This seaweed, thoroughly rinsed, can be used to separate each type of food in the pot. This seaweed is traditionally used (but not mandatory) and adds flavor to your clambake.

Other optional ingredients: Vidalia onions, mussels, or smoked *kielbasa* (Polish sausage).

Photo by Patrice Samara

16

Old-Fashioned Strawberry Shortcake

I love to make this dessert during strawberry picking season. Handmade strawberry picking signs pop up all over Route 27 and on the back roads of East End in June. The strawberries are so sweet and juicy. For those who do not wish to go out into the fields, Pike's Farm, along with many other farm stands in the Hamptons, area sell fresh-picked strawberries daily.

Succulent, fresh strawberries make this dessert a favorite, especially this time of year when the strawberries are abundant and are at their peak.

> 4 cups all-purpose flour
> 4 teaspoons baking powder
> ½ teaspoon sea salt
> 2 sticks (16 tablespoons) unsalted butter, sliced
>   into ½-inch pieces
> 1½ cups milk

Preheat oven to 425 degrees.

In a mixing bowl, add flour, baking powder, salt, and butter slices.

With fingers, pinch butter into flour until it resembles coarse meal. You can do this with a fork, but I prefer my fingers. Now add milk. This is when the dough should be sticky in texture. Don't be concerned. Continue using your fingers turning over the biscuit dough several times and it will smooth out. The key to a good biscuit is not to overhandle. Turn dough in bowl with hands gently for no more than a minute.

On a lightly floured board, gently press dough with the palm of your hand so it spreads out to about to about ¾-inch thick. Using your hands or a biscuit cutter make each biscuit 1 inch thick and about 2½ inches in diameter. You can use the top of a glass 3 inches in diameter to cut the dough if you do not have a biscuit or round cookie cutter.

Roll up scraps and make more. Lightly grease a cookie sheet with butter or shortening.

Bake for 20–30 minutes or until golden brown. Let cool. Cut each biscuit in half just before serving.

Biscuits can be made 1 day in advance and covered in an airtight container and refrigerated. Reheat in a 350 degree oven for 8 minutes to crisp the biscuits.

For strawberry mixture:

> 3 cups cleaned strawberries
> 3 teaspoons sugar
> 2 tablespoons cassis (optional)

In a blender or food processor, add strawberries. Purée until slightly chunky. Add sugar and cassis. Mix with a spoon.

For biscuit top garnish:

> 12 strawberries, sliced in half

Note: If strawberries are not sweet, add more sugar.

For whipped cream:

> 1 pint heavy cream or whipping cream
> 1 teaspoon vanilla
> ¼ cup sugar

In a mixing bowl, add cream. Whip with electric mixer. After 1 minute, when mixture starts to thicken, add vanilla and sugar. Continue beating until cream forms peaks.

Cut biscuits in half. Fill each bottom half with a heaping tablespoon of whipped cream and layer with equal portions of strawberry mixture. Cover with biscuit top. Add a dollop of cream followed by 2 sliced strawberries on top. After assembling, if you have any strawberry mixture left, you can drizzle a little over the top of the biscuits.

Serve immediately.

Beach Picnic
serves 4
Tomato, Peach, and Mint Salad with Champagne *Vinaigrette* • Bonnie's Classic Lobster Roll
Watermelon Wedges with Sliced Nectarines and Figs • Bonnie's Best Chocolate Chip Cookies

When family or friends come to visit us in the Hamptons for a weekend, they always love having local lobster. Believe it or not, there is an ongoing competition regarding where to get the most delicious lobster rolls on the East End.

For over three decades, The Lobster Roll Restaurant in Amagansett has been one of my favorites on the East End. A former clam shack on a dune-lined stretch of Montauk Highway, it is locally known as "Lunch" because of an ancient prominent sign on the roof. Though now serving lunch and dinner, it retains its informal, beachy appeal to locals, celebrities, and vacationers alike.

I have adapted my mother's delicious lobster salad recipe and created a lobster roll that my family thinks is among the best lobster rolls.

Try the salad below to accompany the lobster rolls. When ripe peaches, tomatoes fresh off the vine, and mint fresh from the garden are combined, the flavors are simply delectable! I serve this salad often because it embodies all that reminds me of summer.

Tomato, Peach, and Mint Salad with Champagne *Vinaigrette*

3 large red ripe tomatoes or 5 medium-sized tomatoes
6 ripe firm large peaches
3 tablespoons Champagne vinegar
1 tablespoon extra virgin olive oil
12 mint leaves sliced in thin strips
Fresh ground black or white pepper, about 8 grinds (or to taste)

Wash the tomatoes and peaches. Cut tomatoes in ½-inch wedges. Peel and cut peaches in half. Remove the pit by cutting wedges around it. Cut peaches into ½-inch slices.

Mix all ingredients together and serve.

Bonnie's Classic Lobster Roll

1 pound lobster meat (a 2–2½ pound lobster renders approximately 1 pound of lobster meat)
4 stalks celery (about 1 cup), finely chopped
3 tablespoons mayonnaise (preferably Hellman's)
Juice of 2½ large lemons
1 tablespoon fresh chives, finely chopped
2 teaspoons fresh dill, chopped
4 potato rolls (or hot dog buns)
Pepper and salt, to taste
1 tablespoon salted butter

It can be time-consuming cooking the lobster and picking the meat out. If you have a seafood store or local market selling fresh lobster meat, it is much easier to buy the meat cooked and taken out of the shell. Then it's a cinch to make this classic salad. Ask for mostly lobster tail meat, if possible. The claw meat has a stronger flavor.

If cooking live lobster, you will need approximately a 2–2½ pound lobster to render a pound or more of meat.

Cooking instructions for steamed lobster:

Fill a large pot halfway with water. Bring to a rapid boil and put in live lobster headfirst and cover immediately.

For a 1-pound lobster, cook for 10 minutes; 18–20 minutes for a 2-pound lobster.

When the lobster is cooked (generally, the shell turns bright red), remove lobsters from the pot and let them cool, then remove meat from lobster shells.

Chop lobster meat into ½-inch pieces.

In a medium-sized bowl, add lobster, celery, mayonnaise, lemon juice, dill, chives, pepper, and salt. Mix and add more lemon juice and salt if needed.

A store-bought potato roll is the classic bread used for a lobster roll. If you cannot find a potato roll, use a traditional hot dog bun. The key is to slice a very thin piece of bread off the ends, if it opens in the center.

Preparing the bread:

Heat a griddle or frying pan and melt butter; lightly toast the bottom and top of the rolls about 40 seconds on each side. Remove rolls to platter and mound with desired amount of lobster salad in each roll. Make one lobster roll per person, but I always make a few extra. My husband always has at least two!

Watermelon Wedges
with Sliced Nectarines and Figs

½ watermelon, cut into 2-inch wedges
4 ripe nectarines, remove pit and cut into quarters
1 dozen fresh ripe figs, cut in half
4 sprigs fresh mint

For a festive look, arrange all of the fruit on one oval or round platter with each type of fruit grouped together. Use a few sprigs of mint for garnish. Serve with Bonnie's Best Chocolate Chip Cookies.

Bonnie's Best
Chocolate Chip Cookies

Yield: 24 large cookies

1 cup (2 sticks) butter
¾ cup brown sugar
½ cup sugar
2 eggs
1 teaspoon vanilla extract
2¼ cups unbleached white flour
1 teaspoon baking soda
12 ounces semi-sweet chocolate chips, preferably Ghirardelli chocolate chips (60% cocoa) or any premium baking chips
1 cup walnuts, coarsely chopped

Preheat oven to 350 degrees.

Cream the butter and sugars together with an electric mixer until the mixture becomes light in color. Add the eggs and vanilla. At medium speed, mix very well. Add the flour and baking soda. At low speed, mix until all traces of flour are gone. Fold in the chocolate chips and walnuts.

Drop tablespoonfuls of batter about 3 inches apart onto a greased (with butter or shortnening) baking sheet. Press down lightly. Bake for 10 to 12 minutes or until golden brown.

My Hampton Classic Dinner

serves 4

Pappardelle Portofino with *Pesto* and Tomato Sauce
Veal Chop *Milanese* with Arugula and Tomato Salad • Raspberry Tart

My husband, Nick, adores this preparation of *pappardelle*. He says that it is one of the best pasta dishes he has ever tasted. We had it in Portofino, Italy, at *Ristorante O Magazin*, a small casual restaurant in the old port overlooking the fishing boats that is renowned for the freshest seafood and quality pastas. He loved it so much, we ordered another portion to share! It is so simple and bursting with flavor. This is our adaptation of this dish. We have served this heavenly pasta at several dinners as a first course and received raves.

Pasta Portofino is made with fresh cream, *pesto*, and tomatoes. Basil is a key herb in many Italian dishes and that is why I have always planted it in abundance in my kitchen herb garden. The *pappardelle* is a broad fettucine pasta. Most markets carry a variety of pastas, such as De Cecco Pasta *Pappardelle*.

This Veal Chop *Milanese* with Arugula and Tomato Salad is also one of our favorite dishes. Joan Hamburg of WOR Radio, raved about the Veal *Milanese* Dinner I prepared for her and our friends. She was among the first dinner guests for whom I had prepared this flavorful dish.

Pappardelle Portofino with *Pesto* and Tomato Sauce

Pesto:

- 3–4 bunches basil leaves (about 4 cups of leaves without stems; best to use smaller, tender leaves)
- 1 cup pignoli nuts (pine nuts)
- ½ cup extra virgin olive oil
- 4 large garlic cloves, minced or pressed
- ½ teaspoon sea salt
- 1 cup Pecorino Romano cheese

Purée all ingredients together until creamy smooth. Makes about 2 cups of *pesto*. Can be made up to 5 days in advance.

Garnish:

- 6 basil leaves, sliced into thin strips

Pasta:

- 1 pound *pappardelle* pasta
- 2 teaspoons sea salt

Fill a large stockpot ¾ full with water. Bring to a boil. When water is boiling, add sea salt. Add pasta when ready.

Tomato sauce:

- 3 tablespoons extra virgin olive oil
- 1 28-ounce can imported crushed tomatoes (or 2 large ripe tomatoes)
- ½ cup *pesto* (from recipe at left)
- ½ teaspoon sea salt
- ½ teaspoon white pepper or fresh ground black
- 1 cup heavy cream
- ½ cup Pecorino Romano cheese

In a medium-sized sauté pan, heat olive oil on medium-high heat. When hot, add tomatoes, cook for 10 minutes, stirring occasionally. Lower heat to medium-low. Add *pesto*. Add salt and pepper, if necessary. Cook for another 10 minutes.

Meanwhile, test pasta for doneness, when al dente—chewy but not too soft—remove and drain pasta in colander. Add cream to tomato/*Pesto* sauce. Stir for 2 minutes. Remove from heat.

Note: When you add cream, heat must be low, just enough to heat through, but never boil the cream.

Serve over *Pappardelle*. Sprinkle with grated Pecorino Romano cheese. Garnish with fresh basil strips.

crisp. I sometimes use 2 pans when I prepare them for 8 people. Cook for approximately for 3–4 minutes on each side until golden brown. If bread crumbs are browning too quickly, lower heat. Add more butter and canola oil when needed.

Note: Keep a warm oven at 250 degrees. As each chop comes out of pan, place on a baking sheet in the oven to keep warm. Chops can be left in oven for up to 40 minutes.

When you are finished cooking the chops, place on individual large dinner plates. Using a slotted spoon, partially cascade the chops with the salad (see recipe below).

Arugula and tomato salad:

Arugula is sold fresh at most of the local farm stands during the summer. I go to Jim Pike's in Sagaponack, where he picks arugula daily from his roadside garden. You can buy arugula all year round at many supermarkets.

Pike's, Green Thumb, and Falkowski's Farms' tomatoes are among my favorites. I buy about 6 large tomatoes and let them sit at room temperature for 2 to 3 days so they are extra ripe and abundantly juicy. For better tasting tomatoes, do not refrigerate.

Veal Chop *Milanese* with Arugula and Tomato Salad

3 eggs
2 cups plain bread crumbs
¼ teaspoon cayenne pepper
½ teaspoon sea salt
12 grinds fresh black pepper
3 tablespoons butter, divided
5 tablespoons canola oil, divided
4 rib veal chops, pounded to ¼-inch thick

Preheat oven to 250 degrees.

In a flat bowl or deep dish, add eggs and beat well. Use a dinner-sized plate to blend bread crumbs with cayenne pepper, salt, and black pepper.

In a large sauté or frying pan, heat 2 tablespoons butter and 3 tablespoons canola oil. Heat to a medium-high temperature.

When butter/oil is bubbling, you will be ready to bread your first chop. Dip pounded veal chop in egg mixture, then press lightly into bread crumbs on both sides. Place chop immediately into frying pan. Once you bread them, you must cook them immediately, otherwise they will become soggy. They should be

4 tablespoons balsamic vinegar
6 tablespoons extra virgin olive oil
1 small clove garlic, pressed or finely chopped
2 bunches arugula
2 tomatoes, cut into ¼-inch cubes
1 small red onion, coarsely chopped
Salt and pepper, to taste

In a small bowl, whisk together balsamic vinegar, oil, and garlic to make a dressing.

It is important to wash the arugula well, as arugula can sometimes be sandy. I like to dip it in a bowl of water and swirl it around for a minute or so. Dry on paper towels or in a salad spinner. Cut arugula in half or in thirds, depending on the size of the leaf.

When the veal chops are done, mix all other ingredients in a salad bowl. Add dressing a little at a time. Mix with salad fork or tongs. Add more dressing, if needed. Salad should be lightly coated.

Raspberry Tart

Raspberry Tart is one of the most refreshing, colorful desserts reminiscent of summer. I prefer organic ingredients whenever possible, but they are not necessary.

For raspberry jam glaze:

> ½ cup seedless red or black raspberry preserves

In a small saucepan, heat jam over medium heat for 3 minutes or until melted. Set aside. When pie crust cools, brush bottom with a thin layer of glaze.

For crust:

> *Pâte Brisée* (see recipe on page 45)
> 9- or 10-inch tart pan
> 1 bag dried beans for weight

Make dough and refrigerate for 45 minutes.

Preheat oven to 350 degrees.

Roll out dough so there is a 1-inch overhang on the rim of tart pan. Press gently with your fingers so dough fits into bottom of tart pan and press sides to pan as well.

Now take rolling pin and roll over the top edges of the pan to serrate dough. Peel extra dough off.

With your fingertips, press side edges of dough up so edges are ¼ inch above top edge. This allows room for shrinkage when baking. With a fork, prick the bottom of the pastry shell 4 times.

Cut a piece of parchment paper and place in center of pan. Add 16 ounces dried beans on top of parchment paper and distribute beans evenly around bottom of pan.

Bake for 20 minutes or until top edges are lightly golden. Remove beans and parchment paper and bake for another 5 minutes. Remove and let cool on a rack.

Custard:

> 2 cups organic milk
> 5 egg yolks
> ¾ cup granulated sugar
> ½ cup flour
> 1 tablespoon butter
> 1 tablespoon vanilla extract
> ¼ teaspoon almond extract
> 2 6-ounce packages organic raspberries (about 4 cups)

In a medium-sized saucepan, heat milk but do not boil. About 4–5 minutes.

Place egg yolks in a mixing bowl.

With an electric mixer, gradually mix in sugar (known as creaming). Continue mixing on medium speed until custard turns a light yellow. Slowly beat in flour until blended.

Now gradually beat the heated milk into the egg yolk mixture by pouring it slowly in a stream-like fashion. Beat for another minute.

Pour mixture into saucepan and over medium heat bring to a gentle boil. Whisking will prevent the custard from getting lumpy. If it starts to lump, just whisk faster and the lumps will break up. Cook for 3–5 minutes until custard thickens.

Remove from heat and whisk in butter. Add the vanilla and almond extract and let cool.

The custard can be made up to 1 day in advance and stored in an airtight container and refrigerated.

Otherwise pour custard into the baked pie shell and place raspberries in decorative rows on the top of the tart. Brush raspberries with glaze.

Grilled Veal Chop Dinner
Inspired by Kari Clark

serves 4

Tomato and *Mozzarella di Bufala Napoleon* • Kari Clark's Simply Delicious Veal Chops
Grilled Asparagus • Rustic Ricotta Cheesecake

My dear friend Kari Clark frequently prepares her famous Veal Chops for close friends and family. Kari and her late husband, Dick Clark, the American legend, loved to prepare this dish together at their Malibu home. They always received rave reviews on this dish! Over the years, Kari and I have shared many recipes, and I am deeply honored that she and Dick shared the Simply Delicious Veal Chops for this cookbook.

One of her secrets for a good veal chop is purchasing prime veal from a quality butcher.

Tomato and *Mozzarella di Bufala Napoleon*

This has been a favorite salad and dressing in both my family and Kari and Dick's family for years. The recipe has been passed down from Dinah Shore to Kari Clark to me. The layering of the tomato, mozzarella, and basil makes a dramatic presentation. The veritable flavors of summer burst on the palate… a vine-ripened tomato, fragrant garden basil, and freshly made *Mozzarella di Bufala*. What could be simpler or better?

 4 ¼-inch slices red onion (optional)
 3 large ripe hot-house tomatoes or any large ripe
   tomatoes
 2 balls *Mozzarella di Bufala* (regular mozzarella
   can be substituted)
 12–16 medium-sized basil leaves

Soak red onion slices in a bowl of cold water for 15 minutes. Change water once after 5 minutes. This takes the bitterness from the onions.

On 4 individual plates, place one ¼-slice of tomato on each plate, then layer with a mozzarella slice, 2 leaves of basil, then layer onion, tomato, and one basil leaf on top.

Dressing:

 8 tablespoons extra virgin olive oil*
 6 tablespoons balsamic vinegar*
 ½ teaspoon sugar
 3 teaspoons white wine mustard
 1 crushed or minced large clove of garlic

Whisk ingredients together until smooth and creamy in texture.

Add about 2 tablespoons of dressing on top of each Napoleon and serve.

*Note: Fine extra virgin olive oil and aged balsamic vinegar enhance the flavor of this scrumptious first course.

Kari Clark's Simply Delicious Veal Chops

3 tablespoons butter
4 large cloves garlic
1 bunch fresh sage leaves
4 rib veal chops
Lemon for garnish

Melt butter in small sauce saucepan. Chop garlic and 8–10 sage leaves and add to melted butter. Use this for basting while grilling.

Grill veal to medium or medium rare for best taste (cooking the veal well done can get too dry). Cook about 6 minutes on each side. Baste every few minutes

Serve with a slice of lemon.

Kari's special garnish is to QUICKLY FRY (10–15 seconds at most; you don't want them greasy or overcooked) the leftover sage leaves in very hot oil and serve on top of the chop. The bigger the sage leaves, the better.

Grilled Asparagus

I always cherish the months when asparagus is sold at our local farm stands. They are delectable!

This is a simple yet elegant preparation that can accompany any meat, fish, or poultry dish.

2 bunches green asparagus
¼ cup olive oil
large pinch salt and 6 grinds fresh black pepper, about ⅛ teaspoon

Preheat grill.

Rinse asparagus well and cut off bottom white ends. Use a small sharp knife or vegetable peeler to clean the stalks.

Rub oil on all asparagus. Add salt and lots of fresh ground pepper. Cook on a hot grill for 5–6 minutes (if they are thin, cook less), turning frequently. Using tongs, turn asparagus after a few minutes when you see grill marks. Asparagus should be cooked al dente.

Rustic Ricotta Cheesecake

This is among the best ricotta cheesecakes I have ever tasted; it bursts with creamy ricotta along with a mélange of 2 other flavorful cheeses. I first tasted this extraordinary cheesecake at Porto Cervo restaurant at the Fisher Island Club, Fisher Island, Florida. The head chef, Jesus Benitez, created this version of Rustic Ricotta Cheesecake and it is by far their most popular dessert at the restaurant.

Fresh-made ricotta cheese is always the best. You can find it at most specialty markets. Both *mascarpone* and ricotta are sold at supermarkets, too.

Crust:

- 2 cups flour
- 4 tablespoons (half a stick) butter, cut into ½-inch pieces
- ¼ cup sugar
- 2 eggs
- ½ ounce candied fruit (available in baking section of your local supermaket)

Mix all ingredients, except candied fruit, in either a food processor or by hand in a mixing bowl. If using a food processor, pulse until butter is broken down and all ingredients are blended. Remove and form a ball.

On a lightly floured surface, roll out dough with a rolling pin until ¼-inch thick. Place in a buttered 10-inch springform cake pan. Sprinkle the candied fruit over the dough in bottom of the pan. Wrap a 6-inch high aluminum foil band around the outside circumference of the cake pan. If necessary, use kitchen string to hold foil in place.

Filling:

- 1½ pounds cream cheese
- 1 pound ricotta cheese
- 6 ounces *Mascarpone* cheese
- 12 egg yolks
- 8 ounces sugar
- 1 tablespoon vanilla extract
- 4 egg whites

Preheat oven to 350 degrees.

In a large bowl mix all cheeses, egg yolks, sugar, and vanilla.

In a separate small bowl, beat egg whites until they form peaks. Gently fold whites into cheese mixture and pour into the pan on top of the candied fruit.

Place cake pan in a water bath (¼ of the way up the sides of the pan). Bake for 2 hours.

Turn oven off. Keep cake in oven for an additional 30 minutes. Do not open the oven door to prevent the cheesecake from falling.

If serving the same day, refrigeration is not needed. For future use, cover the cheesecake and refrigerate for up to 2 days.

A Greek Grill Dinner

serves 8

Greek Salad with *Feta* Cheese • Grilled Butterflied Leg of Lamb • *Spanikopita* Casserole
Creamy Rice Pudding with Almonds

When you drive into Bridgehampton, the first thing you see is the famed local meeting place, The Candy Kitchen. The owners, Gus and Aphrodite Laggis, are of Greek heritage. Aphrodite shared her recipes for a favorite dinner she serves to family and guests.

This is a succulent and easy-to-prepare recipe for lamb, as is her *Spanikopita* Casserole. At home, she prepares some of her favorite native dishes from Greece.

When I prepare this Greek dinner for friends, I play some of my favorite Greek music, like "Never on a Sunday" or "Zorba." Great for setting the mood.

I set the table outside on our terrace and use little blue mosaic votive candles and put them all around on the table. If you have small wine or juice glasses, use them to serve the anise-flavored Greek aperitif, *Ouzo*.

Greek Salad with *Feta* Cheese

Greek salad is full of flavor and is a family favorite. It makes a great start to any meal, especially a Greek dinner.

 3 heads romaine lettuce, tough outer leaves discarded
 4 Kirby cucumbers or Persian cucumbers, unpeeled and sliced to ½-inch slices
 12 Kalamata olives, pits removed and cut in half
 2 large ripe tomatoes, cut into ½-inch chunks
 1 small red onion, sliced thinly
 6 tablespoons extra virgin olive oil
 1 teaspoon salt
 Juice of 1 large lemon
 2 tablespoons red wine vinegar
 1 tablespoon dried oregano
 10 ounces Greek *feta* cheese, cut into ½-inch chunks
 ½ teaspoon black pepper, to taste

Wash romaine lettuce and tear each leaf into thirds. I love Kirby or Persian cucumbers because they do not have a lot of seeds and they are full of flavor. In a large salad bowl, add lettuce, cucumbers, olives, tomatoes, and onion.

In a bottle or bowl blend together oil, salt, lemon juice, red wine vinegar, and oregano.

Add half the dressing to the salad and toss gently with salad tongs or a fork and spoon. Add *feta* cubes. If necessary, add a little more dressing at a time, tossing, and taste for lemon, salt, and pepper. Serve on salad plates or bowls.

Grilled Butterflied Leg of Lamb

The key to this lamb is to marinate overnight, which brings out the combined flavors of the garlic, oregano, and lemon.

Then all you have to do is fire up the grill when you are ready to cook. Cook and it is so easy to carve a butterflied lamb.

Serves 8

 1½ cups extra virgin olive oil
 Juice of 4 lemons
 2 tablespoons dried oregano
 3 bay leaves
 10–12 cloves garlic, crushed
 Salt and pepper, to taste
 1 boneless leg of lamb, butterflied

Preheat a gas grill.

For best results, marinate the lamb the day before cooking.

Combine olive oil, lemon juice, oregano, bay leaves, and garlic in a small bowl. Season the mixture with salt and pepper according to taste. Place lamb into a pan and pour mixture over the lamb, coating it well. Tuck the bay leaves beneath lamb. Let lamb marinate for at least 6 hours, preferably overnight, covered and refrigerated.

When ready to cook, preheat the grill. At a low temperature, place the lamb on the grill and brush frequently with the remaining marinade. After about 10 minutes, turn the lamb over. Cook for another 10 minutes until lamb is done to taste. This lamb will be cooked medium rare. Carve in slices.

Serve lamb slices with a square of *Spanikopita* Casserole (see page 33) for each person. Mint jelly is always a popular condiment to serve with lamb.

Spanikopita Casserole
(Greek Spinach Casserole)

    2 pounds fresh spinach
    1 cup scallions, finely chopped
    ¼ cup fresh dill
    2 cups Greek *feta* cheese
    ½ cup extra virgin olive oil
    ¼ cup olive oil for brushing
    1 pound filo dough

Preheat oven to 375 degrees.

Thoroughly wash the spinach, scallions, and dill and dry them completely by using paper towels or a salad spinner. After they are totally dry, place the spinach, scallions, and dill in a large bowl. Add the *feta* cheese and olive oil (more oil may be necessary) to the same bowl and mix. Set aside for 20 minutes.

Brush a 13 x 9 baking pan with olive oil and place 2 sheets of the filo dough overlapping each other along one side of the pan. Make sure that half of the sheets of filo dough are hanging over the edge as well. Brush the dough with a little of the olive oil again.

Turn the pan and repeat the process on the other edges of the pan with 2 more sheets of dough each time on all four sides, brushing each layer with olive oil. Repeat this 7 more times. It seems like a lot of filo dough but keep in mind that the sheets are very thin.

Now, pour the spinach mixture into the center of the pan and spread evenly. Fold the filo dough onto the spinach mixture. Cover the pan with the remaining dough from the package, 8 or 9 sheets. Brush the top again with olive oil.

With a sharp knife, cut through the top layers of the filo dough to make into squares. DO NOT CUT ALL THE WAY THROUGH AT THIS POINT . . . ONLY TOP LAYERS.

Bake the pie for 1 hour or until gold brown. Serve warm or at room temperature.

Creamy Rice Pudding with Almonds

Reverend Dr. Robert Stephanopoulos, once the popular leader of Manhattan's Holy Trinity Cathedral, has been a family friend for over 40 years. I asked him what dessert he liked following a Greek dinner. He proclaimed that he loved rice pudding. So I have included this slightly different twist on everyday rice pudding.

My mother always made rice pudding with rose water or orange water, which is popular in Greek and Mediterraen kitchens. I am not a great fan of the flavors of rose or orange water in rice pudding, so I have omitted them in my version below. You can add it if you like.

    2 quarts plus 2 cups 2% milk
    1 cup granulated sugar
    1 cup Texmati rice
    1 teaspoon almond extract
    2 navel oranges, peel only
    ½ cup raisins (optional)
    2 egg yolks, beaten
    4 teaspoons ground cinnamon
    ½ cup almonds, blanched and slivered

In a large saucepan, add milk and sugar. Bring to a boil. Add rice. Add almond extract, orange peel, and raisins. Lower heat to low simmer, stirring occasionally.

After 30 minutes, remove orange peel and put several spoonfuls of pudding mixture into a small bowl. To this slowly stir in beaten egg yolks. Slowly pour mixture back into saucepan. Add cinnamon and mix well with pudding mixture. Cook for another 15 minutes on low heat until creamy.

Pour into individual serving bowls or one large bowl. Let cool. Garnish with slivered blanched almonds.

Festive Spanish Dinner on the Terrace

serves 6

Gazpacho de Malaga • *Paella Valenciana* • White Sangria • *Flan* with Cognac

The best *gazpacho* I have ever tasted was in Malaga, Spain, at Adolfo Restaurant. It is a blend of all the ingredients usually used in a typical *gazpacho* but with less tomatoes, which allows the flavors of the vegetables to shine and adds a refreshing balance.

During the summer, we go to the local farm stands for our fresh vegetables. This recipe calls for passing the condiments around the table in small bowls, so each guest can add them individually to their *gazpacho*. Passing the condiments adds a festive and authentic touch.

Gazpacho de Malaga

- 2 cups fresh bread, cut into small cubes for croutons
- 8 ripe tomatoes (drop tomatoes into a pot of boiling water for 3 minutes. Drain. Skin should peel off easily. Cut in half and remove seeds.)
- 2 large sweet white onions
- 5 Kirby cucumbers, peeled
- 2 large red bell peppers
- 2 large yellow bell peppers
- 3 garlic cloves, finely chopped or pressed
- 16–18 fresh basil leaves
- 2 teaspoons red wine vinegar
- ½ cup V8 juice
- 4 slices white bread, crust removed
- ½ teaspoon white ground pepper (1 teaspoon if you prefer spicy) or 20 grinds of fresh
- ½ Jalapeno pepper, seeds removed (use rubber gloves or a fork. Do not touch seeds with fingers.)
- 1 teaspoon sea salt
- 1 green pepper

Lightly toast bread cubes in a 375 degree oven for 5 minutes or until lightly brown.

In a food processor, place tomatoes, 1 sweet white onion, 3 Kirby cucumbers, red bell peppers, yellow bell peppers, garlic, basil leaves, vinegar, V8 juice, white bread, white pepper, Jalapeno pepper, and salt.

Purée for about 3–5 minutes until smooth, or use a blender and purée in batches.

Soup should be more salmon colored than deep red.

For Condiment Bowls for Passing:

Finely chop 1 sweet white onion, 1 green pepper, 2 Kirby cucumbers and put in small individual bowls. Put croutons in a small bowl.

Serve *Gazpacho* in soup bowls and pass around condiments bowls, so your guests can add a little of everything. Adding the crunchy vegetables and croutons enhances the blended flavors—adding a delightful texture, pleasing the palate.

Paella Valenciana

¼ cup olive oil
2 dozen large shrimp, shelled and cleaned
6 small lobster tails
3 *chorizo* sausages, sliced in ¼-inch pieces cut
    on the diagonal
6 baby back ribs
1 medium onion, coarsely chopped
5 garlic cloves, minced or pressed
1 teaspoon fresh thyme or ½ teaspoon dried
½ teaspoon cayenne pepper
1 teaspoon sea salt
½ cup white wine
2 cups Uncle Ben's Rice or Spanish short grain rice
1 tablespoon saffron threads (in a mortar, pound
    threads until threads are broken down to
    almost powder) or use 2 packets pre-ground
    saffron, each packet approximately .0044
    ounce. Azafran from Spain is an excellent
    brand of Saffron.
2 cups shrimp broth (see below)
1 cup chopped tomatoes, save juice
3 dozen littleneck clams
8 green olives pitted
6 pimentos, sliced (roasted peppers can be
    substituted)
2 dozen mussels
½ cup clam broth (see to right)

Preheat oven to 375 degrees.

Use a *paella* pan or a shallow round 14-inch pan. *Paella* can be made in a large heavy pot, however a *paella* pan is authentic.

Shrimp broth:

Ask your fishmonger for shells (2 dozen or more) if you purchase the shrimp cleaned. If not, peel shells off shrimp and devein. In a medium-large saucepan add shrimp shells to 5 cups water, one small whole onion, 12 fresh peppercorns, and 6 sprigs of flat parsley. Bring to a boil. Simmer for 2 hours uncovered. Strain.

On medium-high heat, add olive oil to *paella* pan. When pan is very hot, add shrimp. Lightly brown shrimp about 2 minutes on each side. Shrimp should stick to pan before turning. The brown bits that stick to the pan is where most of the shrimp flavor abounds.

Remove shrimp from pan and set aside on a large flat plate or platter. Then add lobster tails and sear quickly for about 3 minutes or until shells turn red. Do not cook all the way. Remove to plate with shrimp.

At this point, if pan is dry, add a little more olive oil.

Add *chorizo* and baby back ribs to pan. Lightly brown for 1 minute on each side. Remove to same plate.

Add onions, garlic, thyme, cayenne pepper, and salt. Stir and cook for 2 minutes.

Add white wine to pan and bring to a boil. After a minute, add rice and stir.

Add saffron, shrimp broth, and tomatoes with juice.

Clam broth:

Fill a medium-sized saucepan with ¾ cup of water and add half of the clams. Cover and bring to a boil. Cook until clams open, about 3–5 minutes. Remove from heat. Pour clam broth into a measuring cup for *paella*. Set aside opened clams.

Stir rice for a minute, then add all seafood on platter, *chorizo*, ribs, olives, and pimentos. Carefully stir into rice.

Add the remainder of the clams and mussels, sticking them into rice so broth almost covers rice. Bring to a boil on top of stove, then immediately place uncovered in oven on the middle rack.

Cook for 45–50 minutes. After 30 minutes, check rice and stir gently. If necessary add a little clam broth (not more than ½ cup).

Note: Clams that do not open should be steamed open in a small saucepan with a ⅓ cup of boiling water. Cover and steam for 3–5 minutes. Discard clams that do not open after steaming.

Cook rice another 10 or 15 minutes until chewy, with a firm texture. Rice should be moist.

It makes a festive and impressive presentation when I bring the *paella* pan into the dining room to show our guests. However, I find it easier to serve on individual plates in the kitchen. Spoon the rice into the center of the plate, followed by some extra clams and mussels and lay the lobster tail next to the *paella* rice. Truly a beautiful dish filled with different textures and colors from the sea.

White Sangria

White Sangria is a nice accompaniment to *paella*.

    2 bottles Spanish or other dry white wine
    1 teaspoon Cointreau
    ¼ cup sugar
    1 apple, sliced
    1 large orange, peeled and cut into wedges
    1 peach, cut into ½-inch slices

Put all ingredients in a large decorative or glass pitcher. Chill for a minimum of 2 hours or more.

Flan with Cognac

    ¼ cup water
    1¼ cups sugar, divided
    2 cups 2% milk
    ½ cup half-and-half
    1 teaspoon vanilla extract
    3 eggs
    5 egg yolks
    2 tablespoons cognac
    Red raspberries, for garnish

Caramel:

In a small sauté pan, add water and 1 cup of sugar. Bring to a boil. Stir and swirl mixture until sugar caramelizes. Sugar should be medium brown when done. Remove from heat and quickly coat the bottom and sides of 6 small ovenproof ramekin custard dishes.

Custard:

In a medium-sized saucepan, heat milk, half-and-half, and vanilla. In a small bowl, whisk together eggs, egg yolks, and ¼ cup sugar. When blended, add to saucepan. Stir to blend into milk mixture. Add cognac. Cook for 3 minutes. Remove from heat and pour over caramel in the ramekins.

In a roasting pan, add water so it comes halfway up the ramekins. Place on lower rack of oven. Cook for 50–60 minutes. Center of custard should have a little movement.

To demold, take a thin, sharp knife and run it slowly around the edge of custard to help it separate from the ramekin. Place a dessert dish on top of ramekin and invert. Tap bottom of ramekin with knife or your hand and lift up. Serve *Flan* on individual plates and garnish with red raspberries.

Summer Lunch by the Pool

serves 4

Grilled Tuna Teriyaki on a Bun with Wasabi Mayo

Grilled Nectarines with Black Raspberries and Vanilla Frozen Yogurt

I had these refreshing sandwiches while in Hawaii many years ago. Of course, fresh tuna is caught daily in Montauk during the season. This grilled tuna sandwich has virtually replaced the burger in our home during the summer and autumn.

Grilled Tuna Teriyaki on a Bun with Wasabi Mayo

    4 tuna fillets, each ¾-inch thick
    ¼ cup bottled teriyaki sauce
    2 teaspoons water
    1 teaspoon wasabi powder
    4 tablespoons Hellmann's mayonnaise
    4 brioche buns or kaiser rolls
    2 medium-sized ripe tomatoes
    4 slices red onion, each ¼-inch thick

Marinate tuna fillets in teriyaki sauce for up to 30 minutes. Reserve marinade.

In a small bowl, add water with wasabi powder and stir until it forms a paste. If it is too dry, add more water. Now add the mayonnaise to the paste and blend together. Mayonnaise should be mildly spicy. If you prefer more zing add more wasabi paste. If too spicy add more mayonnaise.

Heat grill (can broil also).

When grill is hot, grill each fillet for about 3 minutes on each side. Tuna cooks quickly. If you like it rare, cook less. I prefer tuna medium-rare. Brush with teriyaki marinade before turning over. Brush again to keep tuna moist.

Serve each fillet on a bun and top with a slice of tomato, red onion, and wasabi mayonnaise. Serve with pickles, if desired.

Grilled Nectarines with Black Raspberries and Vanilla Frozen Yogurt

    4 large nectarines, cut in half and pitted
    4 tablespoons safflower oil or canola oil
    3 tablespoons Grand Marnier or orange liqueur
    2 tablespoons sugar
    1 pint (2 cups) black raspberries
    2 pints frozen vanilla yogurt

Preheat grill to medium-high.

Brush pitted nectarine halves with oil. Place on grill cut side down and grill for approximately 5 minutes or until they are somewhat soft. Nectarines should be golden and have grill marks. Generously brush the sides and center of the nectarine halves with Grand Marnier Liqueur.

Remove from grill and let cool. Can be done several hours ahead of time.

Black raspberries:

In a small bowl, mix sugar and black raspberries.

Add any remaining Grand Marnier to black raspberries. I sometimes add a tablespoon more which blends well with the flavor of the black raspberries.

Place 2 nectarine halves on each dessert plate. Place 1 small scoop of frozen yogurt in the center of each half. Add a tablespoon of black raspberries on the side of the plate.

Hot August Night Dinner

serves 4

Prosciutto, Melon, and Mint • *Spaghettini* with Arugula and Cherry Tomatoes
Gelato with *Biscotti* and *Vin Santo* (Italian Dessert Wine)

This is a delightful summer pasta for lunch or dinner. While lunching at Capri's well-known beachside restaurant Fontalina, I tasted a light and delicious combination of warm pasta and cold salad. Here is my adaptation of this extraordinary dish of contrasting flavors.

At Pike's Farm in Sagaponack, they grow the sweetest cherry tomatoes. Of course, regular ripe tomatoes can be substituted, but in Southern Italy, the cherry tomatoes were used in most of the salads and pastas. Truly a memorable summer treat.

Prosciutto, Melon, and Mint

A classic Italian favorite is *prosciutto* with melon. I added strips of mint, which brings a fresh twist to this wonderful first course.

> 1 ripe honeydew melon or, when in season, musk melon
> 12–14 mint leaves, sliced thinly
> 1 tablespoon extra virgin olive oil
> ½ pound *Prosciutto de Parma,* thinly sliced
> 4 sprigs mint, for garnish

Cut melon in half and scoop out seeds. With a melon scooper or small ice cream scoop, scoop out balls of melon. Add to bowl with mint and olive oil. Toss lightly.

On four salad plates, lay 3 or 4 pieces of *prosciutto* in the middle of the plate and serve 3 or 4 tablespoons of melon balls on top.

Garnish with mint sprigs.

Spaghettini with Arugula and Cherry Tomatoes

> 1 teaspoon salt
> 1 pound *spaghettini* or spaghetti
> ½ cup extra virgin olive oil
> 2 garlic cloves, crushed
> 2 tablespoons fresh-chopped thyme
>   (1 tablespoon dried)
> Salt and freshly ground pepper, to taste
> ½ teaspoon crushed red pepper (optional)
> 1 cup cherry tomatoes, cut in half
> 2 bunches baby arugula

Fill a large pot ¾ with water and bring to a boil. Add 1 teaspoon salt and *spaghettini.* Stir. Cook until al dente, not too soft . . . still chewy.

In a large sauté pan, add olive oil. On medium-high heat, add garlic and cook about 2 minutes, stirring, so garlic does not brown.

When pasta is done, save 1 cup of pasta water. Drain pasta and add ½ of the *spaghettini* to skillet; add thyme, salt, and pepper. Add more pasta and addi-

tional olive oil, if needed. If too dry, add a little pasta water. Season again for salt and pepper. Add a pinch of red pepper.

In a salad bowl, add cherry tomatoes and arugula.

Dressing:

> 4 tablespoons extra virgin olive oil
> 2 tablespoons balsamic vinegar
> Salt and freshly ground pepper, to taste

Blend all ingredients

Serve hot pasta, about 1½ cups of pasta for each person, in large pasta bowls or rimmed plates and top with salad.

A glass of a cool, crisp Pinot Grigio is a great complement to this dish.

Gelato with Biscotti and Vin Santo

> 8 *Biscotti* (Italian biscuits), 2 per person
> 1 bottle *Vin Santo* (Italian dessert wine)
> 3 pints *gelato* (Suggested flavors: passion fruit, orange, and pistachio. You can substitute with any flavors you prefer. Keep in mind that you'll want to choose a mix of different flavors and colors, which provides a decorative splash on your table!)

This is one of my go-to desserts, because it is so simple in preparation and goes well after eating a filling Italian entrée. In Italy, this is a very popular dessert. There are so many wonderful types of *Biscotti* offered at specialty markets or Italian markets, and I love to serve them along with the fabulous varieties of *gelato* that are now available.

Vin Santo is an Italian dessert wine and can be found in most liquor stores. I recommend purchasing 2 bottles in case your guests are having such a good time they want to linger at the table.

It is customary to serve *Vin Santo* in a small wine glass or liqueur glass.

Farm-Fresh Summer Dinner

serves 4

Adrienne Vittadini's *Penne* with Zucchini • Peachy Cream Tart

This recipe was given to me many years ago by my friend Adrienne Vittadini, and it continues to be a family favorite to this day. I love this recipe for its distinctive flavors, especially when the zucchini is farm-fresh. Adrienne spends much of her time between Water Mill, New York, and Italy. She is renowned for her fashion and design empire, which has spanned several decades.

Penne with Zucchini is delicious and very simple to prepare. I go to Harry Ludlow's Fairview Farm Stand, where he picks fresh zucchini off the vine daily.

Adrienne Vittadini's *Penne* with Zucchini

1 pound small zucchini
6 tablespoons extra virgin olive oil
1 tablespoon unsalted butter
6 cloves garlic, finely minced
1 teaspoon fresh rosemary or ½ teaspoon dried rosemary
1 teaspoon fresh thyme or ½ teaspoon dried thyme
1 teaspoon red pepper flakes
2 pounds *penne* pasta
¼ cup Parmesan cheese
Salt to taste and fresh ground black pepper

I prefer fresh herbs. If using fresh herbs, be sure to use the larger amount.

Wash zucchini and cut into very thin, round slices. Steam lightly and set aside. In a frying pan, heat olive oil and butter. When butter is almost melted, add garlic, rosemary, thyme, and red pepper flakes. Sauté until garlic turns a deep golden brown and has almost a nut-like appearance. Add zucchini and sauté briefly.

Remove pan from heat.

Boil *penne* in salted water according to package directions. Cook pasta al dente.

Toss zucchini/oil mixture with pasta in a large bowl. Add Parmesan cheese and a healthy amount of cracked black pepper, to taste. Continue tossing until Parmesan cheese melts into zucchini mixture.

Serve with additional Parmesan cheese.

Peachy Cream Tart

For many years, my family's favorite peach pie has been from Briermere Farms in Riverhead. Their cream pies are exceptional and always wow my guests. Their recipe has been a family secret for over 25 years. I have never gone a summer without savoring their pies, but I thought it was time I tried to make my own fresh peach cream tart.

I love watching people at the farm stands eating the succulent, fresh peaches at the stand with juices dripping on the ground as they take a bite. The peaches in mid-summer are sold at every farm stand in the Hamptons area. I purchase my yellow peaches (best for this tart) from either Pike's Farm or Crowley's farm stands in Sagaponack. The peaches are fresh picked daily and usually they are hard when purchased. I let them ripen for a day or two on my kitchen counter, so they are ripe but not overripe. This is my version of a Peach Cream Tart.

Pâte Brisée tart crust:
Yield: One ball of dough for one crust

> 1⅔ cups all-purpose flour
> 2 teaspoons sugar
> ⅛ teaspoon salt
> 1 stick (8 tablespoons) butter, cut into thin slices
> 1 egg
> 1 tablespoon ice water (Put an ice cube in a
>   small glass, then add measured water. Use an
>   additional 1 teaspoon water, if necessary.)

If using your hands, in medium-sized mixing bowl, add flour, sugar, salt, and butter pieces. Mix with fingertips and blend until it forms a ball. If using a food processor, pulse flour, sugar, salt, and butter together until it resembles coarse meal, about 1–2 minutes.

In a small bowl, mix egg and water together. Add to flour mixture and knead with your fingers or pulse in a food processor until dough makes a ball. Add a little more water, if necessary.

Make a ball, wrap in plastic wrap, and refrigerate for 45 minutes or up to 24 hours. Before rolling, let stand for 10 minutes if refrigerated for over 45 minutes. Roll dough and line tart pan. Bake per instructions on page 25.

Preheat oven to 350 degrees.

Peaches:

> 8 peaches
> ½ cup sugar
> ½ cup peach jam

When you are ready to fill baked pie shell, peel peaches and cut into ½-inch slices. It is easy to slice around pit starting from top of peach to bottom. Place slices in a bowl. In a small saucepan, heat sugar and jam on low heat for several minutes until blended together. Add to peaches and stir gently.

Cream:

> 2 cups heavy cream
> 8 ounces cream cheese
> ¼ cup sugar
> ½ teaspoon vanilla extract

In a mixing bowl, add heavy cream, cream cheese, sugar, and vanilla extract. With an electric mixer, whip mixture until it is blended well, approximately 2 minutes. On high speed, whip until cream forms stiff peaks.

Now add cream mixture to the pie shell, smoothing it with a rubber spatula or the back of a tablespoon.

Gently top with peaches by laying them side by side on top of cream. Brush additional peach glaze on top peaches. Chill in refrigerator for at least one hour or more before serving. If more than one hour in refrigerator, cover lightly with foil.

Dinner by the Creek

serves 4

Baked Brie • Beer-Can Chicken with Spice Rub
Corn on the Cob with Cayenne Butter • Grilled Zucchini and Eggplant • Blueberry Pie

Beer-Can Chicken is a unique, tasty chicken preparation that has become very popular. The chicken is juicy and moist with a crispy skin. All you have to do is turn on the grill, open a can of beer, and spread the dry rub on the chicken.

Wash the chicken and place the cavity over the can. It looks like the chicken is standing up. To make it easier, you can use a beer-can-chicken roasting pan that has a holder for the can. It can be purchased online or at a gourmet cooking supply store. A baking pan lined with aluminum foil can also be used.

Place on grill as directed and close cover and 45 minutes later, you have a crispy-skinned chicken that is moist and tender!! I usually make two 3½ pound chickens for 4–6 people.

If you want to savor the sweetest corn, then you have to try corn from the East End. Thankfully, cornfields are still in abundance from Westhampton to Montauk. Corn harvested in August is always best. For years I have been using the same foolproof cooking method. It is hard to overcook corn with this recipe.

In our family, we prefer steamed corn served with pats of butter. Another way to serve the corn is with a squeeze of fresh lime juice and sea salt.

Baked Brie

Baked Brie is a favorite *hors d'oeuvre* in our family. I love to serve this especially when we have a birthday to celebrate or a holiday. There is never any cheese left, or bread for that matter.

For 8 or more:

    1 large round sourdough loaf
    1 medium-sized round (32 ounces) of French Brie

Preheat oven to 400 degrees.

With a sharp knife, carefully cut white rind off the Brie. The sharper the knife, the easier it is to cut the rind; be cautious not to take the cheese with the rind. Cut cheese into quarters.

Cut ⅓ off of top of round loaf. With a spoon or a butter knife, scoop out bread from inside, forming a cavity in the loaf. This scooped-out bread should be cut into 1½-inch chunks.

Press Brie into cavity of loaf and bake for 30 minutes. Add bread chunks and top of bread to side of pan around the Brie loaf. This will toast them, which makes it easy for dipping. Bake for another 25–30 minutes. Brie should be bubbling before removing from oven.

Serve.

Beer-Can Chicken with Spice Rub

12-ounce can beer
1 4-pound organic chicken
½ teaspoon turmeric
½ tablespoon Middle Eastern allspice or
    Jamaican allspice
½ teaspoon cumin
1 teaspoon garlic salt
¼ teaspoon cayenne pepper
½ teaspoon sea salt

Preheat grill (side grills only; leave center grill off).

Open can of beer and empty about half of the beer from the can. Wash chicken. Pat dry with paper towel.

In a small bowl, add all spices and salt. Blend together and rub chicken all over; take some of the spices and rub under the skin on the breast, trying to reach as far under the skin as possible. Rub spice mixture inside the cavity.

Place cavity of chicken on the beer can so it is standing upright and place on a beer-can chicken roasting pan or on a small baking pan (I put foil on pan for easy cleanup).

Place chicken on center grill that is turned off. Leave outer grills on medium. Close cover. Check after 30 minutes. Cook for another 15 minutes or until done. If you use a thermometer, it should be 175 degrees. in thigh area. Pull chicken off can, trying not to spill contents of can. Discard can and any remaining beer. Carve chicken and serve.

Corn on the Cob with Cayenne Butter

8 ears corn, shucked and corn silk removed
2 sticks butter
½ teaspoon cayenne pepper

Fill a large pot with water about an inch deep. Lay corn in bottom of pot. Water should not cover corn.

On high heat, bring water to a boil. When water is boiling, cover pot and cook for five minutes. Turn off heat and let sit for up to 45 minutes. The corn will be cooked to perfection. Do not open lid until ready to serve.

Cayenne butter:

Let two sticks of butter sit at room temperature for an hour or until soft. Add cayenne pepper and, using a fork, blend into butter in a small bowl. You can keep the butter in the small bowl or mold into a log. Refrigerate for an hour or until firm. The cayenne butter can be made a day or two ahead, covered and refrigerated.

Grilled Zucchini and Eggplant

 3 small–medium-sized eggplants
 ½ teaspoon salt
 3 green zucchini
 3 yellow zucchini
 3 tablespoons extra virgin olive oil

Preheat grill.

Slice eggplants lengthwise in ½-inch slices. Lay eggplant on a plate in one layer and sprinkle with salt.

Let eggplant sit for 15 or more minutes to give the salt time to absorb some of the water from the slices.

Cut off ends of all zucchini and slice lengthwise in the same manner as the eggplant.

Brush eggplant and zucchini slices with olive oil. Brush grill also with a little oil. Grill slices for about 3–4 minutes on each side. Eggplant and zucchini should be golden with grill marks and soft when done. Vegetables should not be charred. If flame is too high, lower to medium heat.

If you choose not to grill outdoors, you can use either a grill pan on your stove or use the broiler.

Can be cooked ahead of time and covered until ready to use. Reheat in a 375-degree oven for 8–10 minutes.

Blueberry Pie

During the summer months, I make this pie often when the blueberries are abundant and picked daily. The local farm stands sell them as soon as they are picked off the bush.

Pastry dough:

Pâte Brisée—See recipe on page 45. Double the recipe for 2-crust pie (dough needs to be refrigerated for 45 minutes before rolling).

Filling:

 6 cups blueberries
 ½ cup sugar
 ⅛ teaspoon cinnamon
 zest of one medium lemon
 1 egg for egg wash

Preheat oven to 350 degrees.

In a medium-sized bowl, mix blueberries, sugar, cinnamon, and lemon zest.

In a 9-inch pie pan, place rolled out bottom dough and add blueberry mixture. Cover with top dough and pinch bottom dough and top dough together; crimp with the tines of the fork around the edge.

Egg Wash: In a small bowl, mix egg with 1 tablespoon of water. With a pastry brush, brush top and edges of dough.

Place in oven and cook for 50–60 minutes until dough is nicely browned.

Serve with a scoop of vanilla ice cream on the side.

Labor Day Supper

serves 6

Stuffed Zucchini Blossoms • *Percatelli* with Tuna *Caprese* • Seven Layer Ice Cream Cake

There are many ways to prepare zucchini blossoms, and I think this recipe is by far the most delicious. The saltiness of the anchovies along with the mild mozzarella, give the zucchini blossoms an added zing!

First, it is important to get fresh blossoms that are virtually just-picked. Every summer, I prepare these delectable blossoms for *hors d'oeurves*, as well as a first course when entertaining. They are always a huge success. I call Harry Ludlow at Fairview Farms in Bridgehampton to order the zucchini blossoms so he can pick them right before I arrive. I then put them in a plastic bag in the refrigerator until an hour before the guests arrive.

Percatelli with Tuna *Caprese* is virtually my husband and daughter's favorite pasta dish. Durham wheat pasta is essential. The tuna used is not canned tuna, but tuna in a glass jar imported from Italy. There is a big difference in flavor.

I learned how to make this pasta from our dear friend Ralph Galasso. We spent many dinners with Ralph and his wife, Dr. Jane Galasso, in their kitchen cooking up different pastas. A glass of wine in hand, Ralph and Jane always made it look so simple. Together we have always tried to experiment and prepare innovative and delicious dishes.

Stuffed Zucchini Blossoms

24 zucchini blossoms

Rinse each blossom carefully. Remove pistil from bottom of flower.

Stuffing:

1 ball fresh mozzarella
8 or 10 anchovy fillets, each fillet cut into 3 pieces

Cut rectangular pieces of mozzarella into about ¾-inch slices. If the blossom is smaller than that, cut slightly smaller pieces.

Batter:

1 cup of water
1 cup all-purpose flour
½ teaspoon salt
Pinch of cayenne pepper
Safflower oil or canola oil

Add water to flour slowly and mix. Stir in salt and cayenne pepper. Batter should be more of a liquid consistency than pasty. Add more water if needed. This will allow for just a light coating on the delicate zucchini blossoms.

Heat safflower oil or canola oil in a medium frying pan.

Stuff each blossom with one piece of mozzarella and one piece of anchovy. Gently close the petals and softly twist the tips of the flower closed with your fingers and dip into batter. When oil is very hot, add stuffed zucchini blossoms. Fry about 2–3 minutes, turning one time. Should be light golden color. Place cooked zucchini blossom on a paper towel to drain. Remove to a plate and serve.

Percatelli with Tuna *Caprese*

The quality of ingredients is most important in good Italian cooking.

Some members of my family dislike olives and anchovies, but they love the unique blended flavors of this pasta dish! We often have it for lunch with a crisp chilled bottle of rosé wine.

A good Italian market or gourmet store will carry Italian glass-jarred tuna in oil. You need a large pan for tomato sauce, a food processor for the tuna paste, and a large pot of boiling water. In minutes, you will make one of the best pasta dishes ever!

Two 16-ounce boxes *percatelli*—a thick spaghetti with a hole in the center. Can be bought in most supermarkets or specialty markets. De Cecco brand makes a good *percatelli* as well as other types of pasta.

2 balls fresh mozzarella cut into ½-inch cubes. Bring to room temperature before adding to pasta.

Tuna paste:

- 3 8-ounce jars Italian tuna
- 30 black Italian olives, pitted
- 20 anchovies (anchovies in a jar normally contain more than a can. At least 2 cans or jars.)
- ½ cup extra virgin olive oil

In food processor add tuna, olives, anchovies, and olive oil. Purée until all ingredients are blended.

Tomato sauce:

- 3 tablespoons extra virgin olive oil
- 12 cloves garlic, peeled and crushed
- 2 28-ounce cans Italian imported peeled tomatoes
- 1 teaspoon sea salt
- 1 teaspoon red pepper flakes (If you like it spicier, add a touch more, or add less if you prefer it not spicy)
- 8 basil leaves, chopped

On medium-high heat, add oil to a large pan. When oil is hot, add garlic. Lightly brown garlic and make sure oil is very hot before you add tomatoes. Now add tomatoes. You should hear a swish sound when you add tomatoes. Add salt and pepper. Cook and stir for 5 minutes. Lower heat to medium and cook for 10 more minutes. Can be made several days ahead and refrigerated. Otherwise remove from heat until ready to cook pasta.

Bring a large pot filled ¾ with water to a boil. Add 1 tablespoon salt. Now add *percatelli*.

Pasta is done when it is slightly hard but chewy . . . al dente.

While pasta is cooking, add tuna paste to sauce and heat on medium heat. Stir so it blends into the sauce. Add basil. Cook for 3–5 minutes until hot. Stir.

Serve pasta in large bowls or medium-sized plates. Add a generous amount of sauce on top of the *percatelli* and sprinkle mozzarella cubes over sauce. Serve with warm crusty Italian bread.

Seven Layer Ice Cream Cake

Lauren Torrisi, a close family friend, is a classically trained chef and food writer in New York City. She worked in the *New York Times*-rated three-star restaurant kitchens of Colicchio & Sons and Veritas before going to write for ABC News. She has shared a recipe that is adored by grown-ups and kids alike. Everyone loves this multi-flavored ice cream cake made up of everyone's favorite ingredients: devil's food cake, chocolate wafers, strawberry and pistachio ice cream.

    1 devil's food cake (see recipe below)
    1 pint pistachio ice cream, softened
    1 pint strawberry ice cream, softened
    ⅔ cup strawberry jam
    1 cup crushed chocolate wafers

Garnish:

    Whipped cream
    Chopped pistachios

Devil's food cake:

A 9-inch loaf pan

    2 eggs
    ½ cup sugar
    ½ cup sour cream
    1 cup all-purpose flour
    1 teaspoon baking soda
    ½ teaspoon baking powder
    ½ cup cocoa powder
    ½ teaspoon salt
    ¾ cup milk

Note: Bake devil's food cake and assemble the day before serving.

Preheat oven to 350 degrees.

With an electric mixer, mix at medium-high speed the eggs and sugar until it turns pale yellow. Mixture should be creamy and double in size.

With a wooden spoon, fold in the sour cream. Now add the flour, baking soda, baking powder, cocoa powder, and salt. Stir until blended.

Slowly stream milk into mixture. Do not over mix.

Bake cake in a 9-inch greased loaf pan.

Bake for 30 minutes and check by inserting a toothpick into the center of the cake; if it comes out clean, remove cake from oven. If it is still wet, bake for another 10 minutes or until toothpick inserted in center of cake comes out virtually clean. Let cool on a rack.

Assemble the day before: Remove ice creams from freezer and allow to thaw for 30 minutes before assembling cake.

Cut cake into thirds horizontally. Line 9-inch loaf pan with plastic wrap. Place first cake layer in the bottom of the pan.

Spread the softened pistachio ice cream on top of first layer. Now add the crushed wafers on top of pistachio ice cream. Then add the middle layer of cake.

For this layer, spread the cake with strawberry jam and top with a layer of strawberry ice cream. Now top with last layer of cake, and cover with plastic wrap and freeze overnight or until set.

To serve:

Remove cake from freezer. Remove from pan by pulling up on the plastic wrap. Discard plastic wrap and place cake on a platter. Slice and decoratively top with whipped cream and garnish with chopped pistachios. Serve immediately.

Note: Ice cream cake can be frozen for up to one month.

Photo by Lauren Torrisi

Post Labor Day Dinner

serves 4

Avocado, Artichoke, Endive Salad with Shaved Parmesan • Roasted Halibut with Fried Leeks

Mashed Potatoes with *Pancetta* • Grilled Pears with *Mascarpone*

This salad is a simple but impressive first course. The different textures and colors stimulate the palate as well as your eyes.

There is a bounty of varieties of seasonal fish available throughout the year. This recipe calls for halibut. As a substitution, you can use cod or any other white, meaty, non-oily fish.

This was one of the speciality dishes served at the former Della Femina's restaurant in New York. Since my husband was an owner/partner at Della Femina's, I spent many afternoons in the kitchen learning cooking techniques from the chefs. Though there are slight differences, my adaptation has been extremely popular at home.

Even those who claim they do not like fish love this dish!

Avocado, Artichoke, Endive Salad with Shaved Parmesan

Juice of ½ lemon
4 tablespoons fine extra virgin olive oil
1 tablespoon white wine vinegar
1 clove garlic, pressed
Salt, to taste
12 grinds fresh black pepper
16 baby artichokes
2 heads endive
3 ripe avocados, cut in ½-inch slices
12 cherry tomatoes, cut in half
12 very thin slices Parmesan cheese

Four flat salad plates

In a small bowl, add lemon juice, olive oil, vinegar, garlic, salt, and pepper. Mix until blended.

Wash artichokes and take off tough outer leaves. Cut each artichoke in half and with a small sharp knife cut out the choke. I sometimes use my fingers to get out the tiny V-like choke in the baby artichokes. Now cut the halves in half, so you have quarters. Squeeze a little lemon juice on the artichoke to prevent it from turning brown.

Cut ends off washed endive. Cut large endive leaves in half and leave smaller leaves whole.

In a medium-sized salad bowl, add endive, avocado, artichoke, tomatoes, and dressing. Gently toss salad. Taste for salt and pepper.

On individual salad plates, spoon salad on center of plate. You can lay tomatoes on side of dish to give a splash of red color to the plate. The focus is on the avocado, endive, and artichoke.

Lay 3 slices of shaved Parmesan on top of avocado. You may want to serve additional dressing on the side.

Roasted Halibut with Fried Leeks

Leeks:

4 large leeks, cleaned
¾ cup all-purpose flour
1 teaspoon salt
½ cup canola oil

Wash leeks well. Dry with a paper towel. Cut leeks into ¼-inch slices, white and light green parts only. Discard the rest. Dredge leeks in flour and salt in a large Ziploc bag or on a large plate.

Heat a large frying pan with oil. When oil is smoking, add leeks one batch at a time, taking care not to overcrowd. Turn heat down to medium, if necessary. Leeks should be light-medium brown in color. Remove to a paper towel–covered plate to drain. Repeat until all leeks are cooked.

You can prepare leeks 3 hours ahead, and cover with tinfoil until ready to serve.

3 tablespoons canola oil, divided
Prepared leeks
2 tablespoons extra virgin olive oil
4 halibut fillets
Salt and pepper, to taste

Preheat oven to 475 degrees.

In a medium frying pan, heat 2 tablespoons canola oil. When oil is hot add lightly floured leeks. Fry until golden. Put aside on a plate.

Heat a large ovenproof frying pan on medium-high heat. Coat the bottom of the pan with about 2 tablespoons olive oil and 1 tablespoon canola oil. When oil is smoking, add halibut fillets in a single layer. Cook on one side until golden, about 5 minutes. Flip over and remove from heat.

Put the frying pan in the oven and roast for 7–10 minutes.

Serve a generous portion of potatoes (recipe to right) in the center of each plate and top with roasted halibut. Pile a small handful of fried leeks on top of fillet. Spoon a little sautéed mushrooms with truffle oil (recipe on next page) on the side of each plate. And voila! A beautiful presentation and a sure winner with guests or family!

Mashed Potatoes with *Pancetta*

4 medium-large potatoes (preferably Russet)
1 cup milk
3 tablespoons butter
¼ pound *Pancetta,* cubed and fried until crisp
6 sprigs parsley, chopped

Potatoes:

Peel potatoes, cut in half, and put in a large saucepan. Cover with cold water. Boil potatoes until they are cooked, about 25 minutes. Test with a fork. It should go through easily. Drain water.

Add milk and butter to potatoes in pot. Mix and, using a potato masher, mash potatoes. Add more milk if necessary to get the consistency of a smooth and almost runny potato. Add crisp pieces of *pancetta,* and parsley to garnish.

Mashed potatoes can be made 6 hours ahead of time. Refrigerate until ready to use. Adjust for salt and pepper, to taste.

Mushrooms:

  1 tablespoon salted butter
  2 tablespoons extra virgin olive oil
  1 box cremini mushrooms, stems removed and
      caps cut in half (if they are very small, leave
      whole)
  12 *shiitake* mushrooms, stems removed and caps
      cut in half
  ½ cup white wine
  Salt and pepper, to taste
  1 tablespoon white truffle oil
  1 tablespoon parsley, chopped (optional for
      garnish)

Heat butter and olive oil in a large sauté pan. When pan is hot, add mushrooms. Stir for 2 minutes. Add wine and cook for 3 minutes. Salt and pepper to taste. You can prepare this earlier in the day and refrigerate until ready to serve. Heat and add truffle oil just before serving.

Serve halibut on top of mashed potatoes. Then add fried leeks on top of halibut fillets. Place sautéed mixed mushrooms next to halibut fillets. Garnish with parsley, if desired, and serve.

Grilled Pears with *Mascarpone*

Grilling the pears brings out their true flavor. If you do not wish to grill, use either the broiler or a grill pan indoors. This is a simple and lovely dessert to serve. It is light yet flavorful.

  4 Bosc pears
  1 cup *Mascarpone*
  3 teaspoons Grand Marnier or orange liqueur
  6 *Amaretto* cookies, crumbled

Preheat gas grill or grill indoors with a grill pan.

Slice each pear lengthwise and cut out core, scooping out a little extra core to make a bigger pocket for the *Mascarpone*.

Place each pear cut side down on grill. Grill for about 5–8 minutes until pear softens but is not mushy. The grill marks should be visible. Remove from heat. Cover until ready to serve. Can be done 4 hours ahead of time.

Mascarpone cream:

Prepare just before serving. In a small bowl, add *Mascarpone*. Whip with a spoon until creamy. Add Grand Marnier or orange liqueur.

Place 2 pear halves on each dessert plate and fill each pocket with *Mascarpone*. Top *Mascarpone* with a teaspoon of crumbled amaretto cookies or serve whole cookies on the side. Serve immediately.

Optional: Garnish with a sprig of mint, 4 red raspberries, or cookies.

Bonic Seafood Pasta

serves 4

Burrata and *Prosciutto* with Figs • Bonic Seafood Pasta • Orange Sorbet with *Prosecco*

The word Bonic originated from the Bonackers, who lived on the East End of Long Island. The Bonackers are fishermen who emigrated from England in the seventeenth and eighteenth centuries. They settled in East Hampton and the Springs area near the Accabonac Harbor (hence the word Bonackers). They have their own dialect to this day. Though the number of Bonackers has diminished, there are still over 1,500 who reside in the East Hampton area.

Bonackers made their living as baymen, fisherman, and farmers. Clamming of both hard and soft shell clams were at the heart of the Bonac culture and cuisine along with blue crabs and scallops. But since the die-off of the scallops in the 1980s, the scallop industry has never recovered.

Burrata and *Prosciutto* with Figs

2 balls *burrata* (Italian cheese made from cream and mozzarella)
1 pound *prosciutto*
6 ripe figs, cut in half
4 tablespoons fine quality extra virgin olive oil
2 tablespoons balsamic vinegar

Cut each *burrata* ball in half. Lay 3 slices of *prosciutto* in the center of each salad plate. Put each half of the *burrata* on top of the *prosciutto*. Then garnish with 3 halves of figs beside the *prosciutto*.

In a small bowl, blend oil with balsamic vinegar. Drizzle *vinaigrette* over each mound of *burrata*.

As an alternative to the *vinaigrette*, just add a drizzle of extra virgin olive oil The creaminess of the *burrata* coupled with the saltiness of the *prosciutto* can stand alone without dressing, as well.

Bonic Seafood Pasta

My husband and I spent our anniversary several years ago in Positano in southern Italy. A favorite *ristorante* on the beach that is frequented by locals is *La Cambusa*. Their seafood pasta was so fresh and flavorful, as if the seafood came directly from the boat. It left an indelible impression. The memories of our special anniversary flood back when I make this dish.

I had to know what some of the ingredients were, so I asked the owner's wife if they used butter. She told me that it was an extra virgin olive oil from Tuscany and this is what is most important for great flavor in this sauce. A fine extra virgin olive oil from Tuscany and, of course, the fresh sweet cherry tomatoes.

When I returned home to Bridgehampton, I drove to Pike's Farm Stand (still open in October) and bought a pint of their sweet cherry tomatoes, then stopped at The Seafood Shop in Wainscott for the fresh local seafood. I tried to replicate this as closely as possible. If you cannot find a Tuscan oil, any fine quality extra virgin olive oil will do.

> 1 cup fine extra virgin olive oil, preferably one from Tuscany
> 6 large cloves garlic, chopped finely
> 8 large shrimp, shelled and cleaned
> 8 medium-sized calamari (squid), sliced
> 32 cherry tomatoes, cut in half
> 1 28-ounce can San Marzano certified crushed tomatoes
> Salt and pepper, to taste
> Pinch of red pepper flakes (I like 3 pinches)
> 3 dozen littleneck clams
> 3 dozen mussels
> 1 pound spaghetti or linguine
> 6 tablespoons flat parlsey, chopped

Fill a large pasta pot or other large pot ¾ with water and turn on high heat until boiling. Add 1 tablespoon of salt to boiling water.

In a large, deep skillet or medium-sized stockpot, heat olive oil. When hot, add garlic. Wait until the garlic blows up a bit. Do not let it turn brown. Turn heat to high and add shrimp. Cook for 2 minutes on each side and remove to a plate. Add squid slices to skillet; cook for 2 minutes and remove to same plate.

Stir in cherry tomatoes. Cook for 5 minutes. Now add San Marzano certified crushed tomatoes. Stir and cook for 8 minutes. Season with salt, pepper, and red pepper flakes. Now return shrimp and calamari to pan. Add clams and mussels and cover for 4–5 minutes or until clams open. Remove from heat.

Add pasta to boiling water and stir. Cook until it is al dente. Most dry pastas take about 6 or 7 minutes. Tasting the pasta after 5 minutes is always the best barometer.

Drain when done. Serve in pasta bowls or deep plates and spoon with seafood sauce. Try to divide seafood equally. Sprinkle with chopped parsley and serve.

Tip: Spoon a little sauce over pasta first and mix into pasta. Then finish off with seafood and more sauce. This insures that all the pasta is coated with sauce.

Orange Sorbet with *Prosecco*

1 pint orange sorbet
1 cup *Prosecco* Italian dessert wine, divided
16 red raspberries
8 *Biscotti*

In 4 separate dessert bowls (a shallow, stemmed glass or goblet works well) put 2 scoops of sorbet, ¼ cup of *Prosecco* and 4 raspberries.

Serve with *Biscotti*.

Autumn Menus

James Brady's Apple-Smoked Steak Dinner–serves 4
James's Favorite *Vinaigrette* Salad • Apple-Smoked Grilled Steak • Bridgehampton Potato Gratin
Orchard Apple Pie

Indian Summer Lunch–serves 4
Chopped Salad with Roasted Peppers and Blue Cheese
Mussels with Lemongrass and French Fries (*Moules Frites*) • Mixed Berries with Yogurt Cream

Sunday Supper on the Terrace–serves 6 to 8
Mesclun Salad • Pasquale's Eggplant Parmigiana

Candlelit Saturday Night Dinner–serves 4
Pomegranate and Pear Salad • *Osso Bucco* with *Gremolada* • *Risotto Milanese* • *Gelato* Trio

Sunday Meatloaf Dinner–serves 6
French Onion Soup • Sunday Meatloaf for Six • Buttered Parsley Noodles • Peas and Carrots
Old-Fashioned Banana Split • Chocolate Sauce

Spaghetti with Veal Meatball Dinner–serves 4
Avocado and Hearts of Palm Salad • Veal Meatballs and Spaghetti
Marinated Orange Sections in Grand Marnier

From the Sea – Gerard Drive Fish Soup by Pierre Franey–serves 6
Boston Lettuce Salad with Mustard *Vinaigrette* • Gerard Drive Fish Soup by Pierre Franey
BAV's Herbed Stuffed French Bread • Autumn Plum Tart

Thursday Night Dinner–serves 4
Kristin's Guacamole and Chips • West Coast Chicken Tortilla Soup
Shrimp Tacos with Mango and Avocado Salsa • Margarita Cocktail • *Madeleines*

New Orleans-Style Barbecue Shrimp Lunch–serves 4
Tomato, Cucumber, and Mint Salad • New Orleans-Style Barbecue Shrimp
Carmelized Banana Walnut Tart with Almond Butter

Autumn Saturday Dinner for Eight–serves 8
Queensland Blue Pumpkin Soup with *Crème Fraîche* • Rib Pork Chops with *Gorgonzola Dolce* and Figs
Peas and Pearl Onions • Fingerling Potatoes • Gingersnap Cake with Lemon Cream

Pre-Thanksgiving Dinner–serves 6 to 8
Tomato, Red Onion, Basil with Balsamic *Vinaigrette* • Lobster and Shrimp *Fra Diavolo*
Poached Pears with *Gorgonzola Dolce*

Thanksgiving Dinner with Free-Range Turkey–serves 12 (with leftovers)
Shrimp *Bisque* • Roast Turkey • Spiced Sausage Nut Stuffing • Cranberry Chutney with Mango
Fennel *au Gratin* • Brussels Sprouts with *Pancetta* • Baked Glazed Yams with Pecans
Spiced Pumpkin Pie with Whipped Cream

James Brady's Apple-Smoked Steak Dinner
serves 4
James's Favorite *Vinaigrette* Salad • Apple-Smoked Grilled Steak • Bridgehampton Potato Gratin
Orchard Apple Pie

James Brady was a renowned journalist and marine novelist who spent many weekends throughout the year at his country home in East Hampton. A legend at the *New York Post,* James was the first editor of *Page Six.* When he was not writing his weekly columns in *Parade* magazine, *Advertising Age,* or one of his many novels, James enjoyed entertaining his family and friends at his home on Further Lane.

For over twenty years, my husband and I shared many wonderful evenings with James in both East Hampton and New York.

One of his favorite steak recipes came from a carpenter he met at a popular local watering hole in East Hampton, the Blue Parrot restaurant. It was simple and delicious. He served it with green garden salad and cold pasta with *pesto.* James went to the popular Villa Italian Specialty Store in East Hampton, where he purchased his vinegar, oil, and their homemade *pesto* sauce. He used the *pesto* on *penne* and made the pasta ahead of time and refrigerated it until an hour before serving.

Villa Italian Speciality Store has been a mainstay on the East End for over 20 years. (See *Pappardelle Portofino* on page 22 for my *pesto* recipe.)

James's Favorite *Vinaigrette* Salad

James Brady had his favorite extra olive oil and vinegar. Quality ingredients are the key to successful cooking and James's thorough knowledge of sources and quality were evident in his choices. First-pressed olive oil has the best flavor.

He told me he would make this dressing often because everyone loved it and it was known as James's Signature Dressing.

> 6 tablespoons Colavita 1st pressed extra virgin olive
>   oil (any extra virgin olive oil can also be used)
> 2–3 tablespoons red wine vinegar
> ½ teaspoon Coleman's dry mustard
> ½ teaspoon dry thyme
> ½ teaspoon dried rosemary
> ½ teaspoon garlic chips or 2 small cloves, pressed
> ½ teaspoon salt
> Fresh ground pepper, to taste
> 1 head romaine lettuce, torn into thirds
> 1 head Boston lettuce, torn into thirds
> 3 stalks celery, sliced into ¼-inch pieces
> 1 large tomato, cut into ½-inch pieces
> ½ small red onion, sliced
> ½ bunch flat parsley, leaves only, chopped
> 3 Kirby cucumbers sliced, ¼-inch thick

In a bowl or salad dressing jar, whisk together first eight ingredients. Dressing can be made up to 3 days ahead and kept in the refrigerator. Shake well or whisk before using.

Wash lettuce and dry in a spinner or on paper towels. I always wash lettuce ahead of time and wrap in paper towels and refrigerate until ready to use. You can do the same for the other vegetables. Keep chopped tomato in a separate small bowl if you prepare vegetables ahead of time.

In a salad bowl, add lettuces, celery, tomato, red onion, parsley, and cucumbers. Add 4 tablespoons of dressing. Toss salad several times to mix. Taste for salt and pepper. This salad is best when served chilled.

Apple-Smoked Grilled Steak

    1 tablespoon garlic powder
    Fresh ground black pepper
    3 tablespoons Worchestershire sauce
    4 sirloin steaks (one per person)
    2 tablespoons kosher salt
    1 bunch apple tree branches (or apple barbecue
        wood chips)

Sprinkle garlic powder, pepper, and Worcestershire sauce on the steaks 10 minutes before grilling. When ready to grill, sprinkle steaks with kosher salt.

Heat grill for ten minutes on high or until coals are hot. Place cut-up apple tree branches either in a smoke box or directly on the coals, as James preferred. After a few minutes, grill steak; depending on size, grill until firm to touch in center. Should be about medium rare. Let steak rest 5–10 minutes before serving.

Bridgehampton Potato Gratin

I serve his tasty steak and potato gratin with Art Ludlow's fresh-made Gruyère cheese.

    4 large baking potatoes, thinly sliced
    1½ cups 1% or 2% milk
    ½ cup half-and-half
    2 scallions, finely chopped
    2 large garlic cloves, pressed or finely chopped
    ½ teaspoon salt
    ¼ teaspoon pepper
    ¼ teaspoon fresh grated nutmeg, preferably, or
        ground
    1 teaspoon flat parsley, chopped
    1 cup Gruyère cheese, grated or thinly sliced

Preheat oven to 375 degrees.

Combine sliced potatoes, milk, half-and-half, scallions, garlic, salt, pepper, nutmeg, and parsley in a medium-sized saucepan. Cook for 7 minutes on medium-high heat.

Add ¼ of potato mixture to an ovenproof oval porcelain baking dish or gratin dish. Add ⅓ of cheese over the potatoes, then layer again with potato mixture and cheese until finished.

Bake until golden brown on top, about 40 minutes. If not brown after 45 minutes, raise oven temperature to 425 degrees for 5 minutes.

Orchard Apple Pie

After Labor Day, the crowds are gone on the East End. Suddenly the air is crisp, and driving east on Montauk Highway, signs begin popping up saying "Pick Your Own Apples." Our Orchard Apple Pie exemplifies autumn to me.

9- to 10- inch pie pan

Double *Pâte Brisée* dough recipe on page 45.

Make at least 1 hour ahead.

    5 medium Granny Smith apples or other tart
        apples
    3 Fuji or any other semi-sweet apples
    ½ teaspoon ground cloves
    2 tablespoons ground cinnamon
    Zest of half a small lemon (grate yellow part only,
        not white pith)
    1 cup sugar
    1 tablespoon sweet butter, cut into 4 pieces
    1 egg yolk (for egg-wash glaze)

Peel apples and slice into ½-inch thick slices. In a large mixing bowl, add apple slices, cloves, cinnamon, and lemon zest.

Preheat oven to 400 degrees.

On a floured work surface, roll out 1 ball of dough at a time to fit the pie dish. Roll from the center out. Keep turning to roll evenly. The top dough should overlap the sides of the dish by an inch.

Lay bottom dough in pan. Press gently with hands to be sure that dough fits well into the bottom.

Mix sugar into the spiced apple mixture. With a large spoon, evenly distribute apples. Dot with butter and cover with top layer of dough.

Pinch sides of bottom and top dough together. Using the tines of a fork, press against the front side of trim to give it a finished look.

Beat egg yolk until well blended.

With a fork, make a few puncture marks in dough or carving the first letter of your first or last name is fun. Brush top and trim with egg yolk.

Bake for 50–60 minutes until crust is golden.

Indian Summer Lunch

serves 4

Chopped Salad with Roasted Peppers and Blue Cheese

Mussels with Lemongrass and French Fries (*Moules Frites*) • Mixed Berries with Yogurt Cream

The best *moules frites* I ever tasted was at a small café in the main square in Brussels, Belgium. It was the only item that they served. Of course, I have tried to duplicate their dish with some success, with the exception of their fries. I know that in France and Belgium, they usually fry the fries twice. If you have an electric deep fryer with a basket, this is an easy process. If you don't have an electric deep fryer, a frying pan will suffice. You can also serve the mussels as a first course.

Chopped Salad with Roasted Peppers and Blue Cheese

Most supermarkets carry a wonderful variety of organic mixed greens all year round. The roasted red peppers and a hint of blue cheese add a flavorful twist to a great chopped salad.

  2 roasted red peppers (see instructions next
      column)
  1 large head romaine lettuce
  ½ red onion
  2 ripe tomatoes, chopped
  ¾ cup blue cheese, crumbled
  5 tablespoons extra virgin olive oil
  2 tablespoons white wine vinegar
  ½ teaspoon salt
  ½ teaspoon freshly ground black pepper

Roasting peppers:

Preheat oven to 500 degrees.

Place red peppers on a rack in the oven. Place a roasting pan filled half way with water beneath the rack. Cook peppers, turning occasionally, for 20–30 minutes until skin is almost slightly charred. Remove from oven. Let cool slightly; peel skin off and discard. Cut red peppers in half, remove seeds, and chop.

Separate and wash lettuce leaves, discarding large tough leaves. Finely chop leaves. Finely chop red onion.

In a salad bowl, add all vegetables and blue cheese. In small bowl, blend oil, vinegar, salt, and pepper. Add half of dressing to salad. Mix and taste. If dry, add the rest of dressing. Taste for salt and pepper.

Mussels with Lemongrass and French Fries

(Moules Frites)

Mussels can also be served as a first course.

> 3 tablespoons extra virgin olive oil
> 3 tablespoons lemongrass, finely chopped
> 3 tablespoons scallions (white and lower part of
>   green stalk), chopped
> ¾ cup white wine
> 1¼ cups coconut milk
> 3 pounds large mussels
> 1 tablespoon cilantro, chopped
> ⅛ teaspoon cayenne pepper

Coat bottom of large pot with olive oil. Heat oil and when it is hot, add lemongrass and scallions. Cook for 2 minutes and stir. Add white wine. Cook for another 2 or 3 minutes. Add coconut milk. Stir. Add mussels. After 3 minutes, add cilantro and pepper. Mix gently with mussels. Cover and cook for another 2 minutes until mussels open.

Serve immediately in large bowls.

French fries:

> 1 cup canola oil
> 4 large Idaho potatoes
> Salt

Heat oil on medium-high heat in a large frying pan.

Cut each potato in half lengthwise. Now cut again lengthwise into quarters and cut quarters in half. If you like them thinner, cut lengthwise again. Lay slices on paper towels and pat dry.

When oil is lightly smoking, add dry potatoes in a single layer to oil. Place golden potatoes on a paper towel when removed from pan to absorb excess oil. Repeat until all potatoes are cooked. Salt to taste. Serve hot.

Mixed Berries with Yogurt Cream

16 ounces 2% low-fat Greek yogurt, most Greek
    yogurts like Fage brand are strained
10 ounces low-fat vanilla yogurt
5 tablespoons organic honey
4 sprigs mint

Berries:

2 cups blueberries, organic preferably
2 cups raspberries, organic preferably
2 cups hulled strawberries, organic preferably
¼ cup sugar

Wash the berries and drain in a colander or on paper towels. Hull the strawberries. Allow to air dry for 30 minutes. This can be done earlier in the day. Slice larger strawberries in half.

In a medium-sized bowl, add berries and sugar. With a wooden spoon, gently blend sugar with berries. Refrigerate until ready to use.

Mix the two different yogurts together in a bowl. Put yogurt in a large sieve or cheesecloth over bowl and allow liquid in yogurt to drain for up to four hours, or squeeze liquid out in a paper towel or cheesecloth. If you do not have a sieve or cheesecloth, paper towels will work. After 3 hours, squeeze any excess liquid out and add yogurt to a dry bowl. Yogurt should have a thicker, creamier consistency. Mix yogurt. Add honey. Mix and refrigerate until ready to use. Can be made 1 day ahead.

Serve in glass or porcelain dessert bowls. First add several heaping tablespoons of yogurt cream and top with berries. Garnish with a sprig of mint.

Sunday Supper on the Terrace

serves 6 to 8

Mesclun Salad • Pasquale's Eggplant *Parmigiana*

I love this classic version of Eggplant *Parmigiana*. Pasquale Anthony Pagnotta has lived between New York and East Hampton for over twenty-five years. His creative talent in home design carries over to his talented cooking abilities. Always entertaining clients and friends, Pasquale is an avid cook, and he shared one of his favorite meals that he serves when entertaining at home.

Mesclun Salad

5 tablespoons extra virgin olive oil
2 tablespoons white balsamic vinegar
¼ teaspoon sea salt
¼ teaspoon fresh ground pepper
2 containers (approximately 6 cups) mesclun, preferably organic
3 celery stalks, cut into ¼-inch pieces
2 carrots, peeled and cut into ¼-inch slices
3 Kirby cucumbers, sliced in ¼-inch pieces
½ small red onion, thinly sliced
Salt and fresh ground pepper, to taste

In a small mixing bowl, blend together olive oil, vinegar, salt, and pepper. Dressing can be made one day ahead.

Prepare salad ahead. In a large salad bowl, add vegetables. Refrigerate until ready to serve.

When ready to serve, add half the salad dressing. Mix with salad tongs. Taste for salt and pepper. If needed, add more dressing.

Pasquale's Eggplant Parmigiana

This is a favorite dish among eggplant lovers. Pasquale serves this excellent Eggplant Parmigiana for an afternoon lunch on his patio.

Eggplant Parmigiana can be served as a first course or for an entrée.

Crusty herb bread goes well with this classic Italian dish.

Pasquale prepares and bakes this casserole a day before he serves it. Cover and refrigerate overnight. He claims it is even better the next day.

Pasquale's tip: Remove from refrigerator and cut the eggplant into squares while it is cold, and reheat it. He found when cut cold, the eggplant squares remain firm with straight lines. *Molto bene!*

2 large eggplants
2 tablespoons Kosher salt
1 28-ounce can imported Italian plum tomatoes, preferably San Marzano
2 cloves garlic, peeled and minced
1¼ cups extra virgin olive oil, divided
½ cup all-purpose flour
½ cup fine dry breadcrumbs, preferably homemade (take day-old Italian or French bread and chop it in a food processor for 1 minute or until it is the size you want)
8 large eggs, beaten
¼ cup canola oil
1½-pound ball fresh mozzarella, sliced into ¼-inch pieces.
1 cup Parmesan Reggiano, freshly grated
12 grinds black pepper
20 basil leaves, cut into strips

Cut eggplants lengthwise into ¼-inch slices. On a large cookie sheet, lay slices side by side and sprinkle with Kosher salt or regular salt. This absorbs much of the liquid inside the eggplant. Lay a few plates on top of eggplants to weigh them down. Leave for at least 1 hour, up to 2 hours.

After one to two hours, press down on plates to help squeeze any excess water from eggplant slices. Now lay the slices on paper towels.

Prepare tomato sauce.

Combine tomatoes, garlic, and ½ cup extra virgin olive oil in a food processor. Salt and pepper to taste. Set aside.

Preheat oven to 350 degrees.

In a wide, shallow bowl or deep plate, combine flour and breadcrumbs. In another shallow bowl, beat eggs.

Heat canola oil and remaining olive oil in large, deep skillet over medium heat. The oil should be about 1 inch deep. When oil is simmering, dredge eggplant slices in the flour, then in the egg, and then into the frying pan. Do not overlap.

Fry in batches. Have a large plate ready with a paper towel for eggplants to drain when done. With a kitchen fork, turn slices over when golden, about 1–2 minutes per side. Remove slices and allow to drain on paper towels. Repeat until all slices are done.

Spread 1 cup of tomato sauce on bottom of casserole dish. Top with a third of the eggplant slices. Top eggplant with half of the mozzarella slices.

Sprinkle with a generous amount of Parmigiano Reggiano cheese, and freshly ground pepper and ⅓ of the basil leaves. Now add another layer of eggplant slices, top them with a cup of tomato sauce, remaining mozzarella, half of the remaining Parmigiano Regginano cheese, all of the remaining basil leaves. Add remaining eggplant slices and top with remaining sauce and remaining cheese. Bake until cheese has melted and top is light brown, about 30 minutes. Allow to rest 10 minutes prior to serving.

For Dessert:

Pasquale serves a simple dessert of sliced pears, grapes, and *Biscotti* with a cup of espresso.

Candlelit Saturday Night Dinner

serves 4
Pomegranate and Pear Salad • *Osso Bucco* with *Gremolada* • *Risotto Milanese* • *Gelato* Trio

During the high season on the East End, there is a busy summer schedule, like many ocean resort areas. But those of us who spend weekends year 'round in the Hamptons share a special secret . . . chilling out in front of the fireplace and having intimate dinners, when the crowds have gone.

Pomegranate and Pear Salad

2 heads bibb or boston Lettuce
½ pomegranate, seeds only
2 Bosc pears
Juice of ½ lemon
3 tablespoons extra virgin olive oil
2 tablespoons balsamic vinegar
½ clove garlic, pressed
Salt and pepper, to taste

Wash lettuce and spin dry in a salad spinner or on paper towels to air dry. Discard outer tough leaves. Tear or cut lettuce leaves in half, larger ones in thirds.

Cut pomegranate in half. With a small fork, take out seeds and separate from white veins; place seeds in a small bowl.

Cut off stem and bottom of Bosc pears. Leave skin on and cut into ¾-inch slices, avoiding or removing the core as you go. Set aside on a plate and sprinkle with lemon juice to keep from turning brown.

In a small bowl, blend oil, balsamic vinegar, and garlic.

In a salad bowl, mix lettuce and half the pomegranate seeds with dressing. Add salt and pepper to taste. Add pear slices and toss once or twice. Place lettuce mixture in the center of a salad dish. Sprinkle salad and pears with remaining pomegranate seeds and serve.

Osso Bucco with Gremolada

  2 tablespoons olive oil
  4 veal shanks 1½–2 inches in height, ask your
      butcher to tie each one with string
  ¼ cup white flour
  3 small carrots
  1 medium onion
  4 stalks celery
  1 cup red wine (for deglazing)
  3 tablespoons butter
  6 cloves garlic, pressed or finely chopped
  1 cup whole peeled canned tomatoes,
      chopped, save juice
  ¾ cup beef broth
  ½ teaspoon dried thyme
  1 teaspoon dried marjoram
  1 bay leaf
  Small pinch of cayenne pepper
  3 strips orange peel
  1 strip lemon peel
  1 teaspoon salt, plus small amount for seasoning
      veal
  ½ teaspoon freshly ground black pepper, plus
      small amount for seasoning veal
  ½ cup water, if needed

Preheat oven to 350 degrees.

In a large Dutch oven or a heavy pot that can go from stove to oven, heat oil on medium-high heat (enamel pots are ideal). While oil is heating, roll each veal shank in flour. Sprinkle with salt and pepper. Cook until medium brown on all sides, about 12 minutes. It is important to stand them on their sides so that all areas are browned. While meat is cooking, prepare vegetables.

Using a food processor makes this dish easy to prepare. Process carrots until finely chopped. Remove carrots and put in a small bowl. Follow the same procedure with onions and celery and add them to the same bowl.

When veal shanks are browned, remove to a platter. Remove any excess fat from the pot. Add wine and scrape sides and bottom to loosen brown bits. This is an important step in cooking this dish, because the flavor of the meat is in these dark bits stuck to the pot. After wine cooks off (about 3 minutes), add butter. When butter is melted, add prepared vegetables, then garlic. Cook until soft (about 7 minutes).

Now place veal on top of vegetables side by side, not overlapping. Add tomatoes, broth, thyme, marjoram, bay leaf, cayenne pepper, and fruit peels, along with salt and pepper. Gently blend ingredients around veal. Broth should cover meat. If it does not, add ½ cup water. Heat for 5 minutes on top of stove until broth is boiling. Cover pot and place in the preheated oven.

Cook for 2–2½ hours, until meat is about to fall off bone. Check after 1 hour; if broth evaporates to where it is covering less than ¾ of each shank, add a little more broth. When done, remove bay leaf and fruit rinds.

Place veal shanks on platter. Cover with aluminum foil and keep warm. Meanwhile, boil down broth until it thickens.

Cut string off each shank (if tied) and discard. Serve veal shank on top of *Risotto Milanese* (recipe below). Add vegetable sauce on top of each veal shank. Sprinkle *Gremolada* (recipe below) on center of the veal shank bone.

Gremolada:

The traditional recipe for *Osso Bucco* is made with a garnish of finely chopped parsley, grated lemon peel, and lots of finely chopped garlic. Since the flavor of raw garlic can be overpowering, I sprinkle it over the marrow in the center of the veal shank bone. The contrast of colors makes a lovely presentation.

  4 tablespoons flat parsley, finely chopped
  1 lemon peel, grated
  2 garlic cloves, finely chopped

Mix all ingredients together and sprinkle ½ teaspoon of the *Gremolada* on top of each veal shank.

Risotto Milanese

  4 tablespoons sweet butter, divided
  ½ cup onion, finely chopped
  3 cans (6 cups) chicken broth or homemade
      chicken stock
  ½ cup dry white wine
  1½ cups fine Arborio rice
  1 teaspoon saffron threads or ¼ teaspoon saffron
      powder
  ¾ cup Parmesan cheese, freshly grated
  Salt and pepper, to taste

In a heavy-bottomed saucepan, melt 1 tablespoon of butter over medium heat. Add onion. Cook until onion is pearly white in color, almost translucent, about five minutes. Meanwhile heat broth in a separate saucepan. Bring to a boil, then lower heat to simmer. Add wine then rice to onions. Stir while heating for about two minutes.

With a soup ladle (a large soup ladle usually measures about ½ cup of liquid, ideal for this use), spoon a ½ cup broth into the *risotto*. Stir with a wooden spoon. Add another ½ cup of broth when most of broth has boiled down, about two minutes. Repeat this step until *risotto* is almost done. Maintain heat at a medium to medium-high level. A steady slight boil is best. Stirring continually, taste *risotto* after cooking for 17 minutes. The *risotto* should be al dente or slightly hard in the middle.

In a small cup or bowl, mix saffron with ½ cup hot broth. I prefer to use saffron threads for freshness. I crush them in a mortar. Add saffron and broth to *risotto*. Stir. Add another ladle full of broth and cook for another minute.

Turn heat off.

Add another two ladles full of broth and the remaining 3 tablespoons of butter and stir. Add ¾ cup freshly grated Parmesan cheese. Salt and pepper to taste. At this point, the *risotto* should resemble a thick soup. But don't be deceived. The broth will be mostly absorbed by the time you plate it with the veal. If your preference is a more moist *risotto*, add a little extra hot broth.

Shortcut: Two or three hours before dinner, cook *risotto* halfway. Use above recipe. Cover and set aside. When *Osso Bucco* is done and ready to be served, you can begin to finish cooking *risotto*. *Risotto* will be almost ¾ of the way done at this point. Bring remaining broth to a boil. Heat *risotto* slowly in pot on low heat at first and keep stirring. After a few minutes, stir in simmering broth. Add saffron to broth, as instructed above, then to *risotto*. Stir and follow last steps in recipe. Add remaining butter, mix in cheese, salt, and pepper to taste. If necessary, add another ladle or two of broth until *risotto* is smooth and somewhat soupy.

To reheat, cooking time should be about 5 minutes.

Gelato Trio

There is nothing more refreshing than a *gelato* trio after a heavy meal. The key is to create a splash of colors with an assortment of flavors. There are many different flavors now sold at the supermarkets and specialty markets. You choose. A few of my favorites are lemon, raspberry, and mango.

Add a sprig of mint to each plate and *voila!*

If you really want to wow your family or guests, serve the 3 scoops on long narrow white dishes.

> Medium-sized ice cream scoop
> 1 pint mango *gelato*
> 1 pint lemon *gelato*
> 1 pint raspberry *gelato*
> 4 sprigs fresh mint

Serve. Pass a cookie platter or 3-tiered dessert caddy around the table with an assortment of cookies and chocolates.

77

Sunday Meatloaf Dinner
serves 6
French Onion Soup • Sunday Meatloaf for Six • Buttered Parsley Noodles • Peas and Carrots
Old-Fashioned Banana Split • Chocoate Sauce

My husband, Nick's, favorite dinner is meatloaf. It has become a Sunday ritual in our home while watching football during the autumn. I love shaping the meatloaf like a football! Surround it with Buttered Parsley Noodles and watch everyone's mouth water when you bring it to the table.

There are many types of onions available at this time of year from the farm stands. Sweet onions are preferable in this French Onion Soup recipe. I purchase my onions at Pike's Farm in Sagaponack. During the year, I buy Vidalia onions or any other sweet onions.

French Onion Soup

3 tablespoons unsalted butter
1 tablespoon extra virgin olive oil
2 large sweet onions, thinly sliced
Pinch of sugar
4 cups organic beef broth
1 cup water
1 tablespoon Cognac
1 French baguette, cut into ½-inch slices for
    croutons, lightly toasted
1 cup aged Gruyére cheese, thinly sliced. Use
    a cheese slicer or sharp knife. Cut into 2- or
    3-inch slices.
3 tablespoons parsley, finely chopped
6–8 ovenproof soup bowls (can be purchased at
    stores such as Williams-Sonoma)

Preheat oven to 400 degrees.

In a medium-sized heavy pot on medium-high heat, melt butter with olive oil. When butter starts to bubble, add onions and a big pinch of sugar. Stir occasionally until onions turn a medium-brown color, approximately 10–15 minutes. Stir in broth, water, and Cognac.

Lower heat to simmer. Cover partially, leaving top slightly opened. Cook for 30–40 minutes. Can be made a day or two in advance.

When ready, spoon soup into ovenproof bowls. Add 2 or 3 pieces of crouton slices. Quickly lay Gruyére cheese slices on top of croutons. The croutons help to keep the cheese from sinking into the soup. Bake for 20 minutes until cheese is melted and lightly browned. Sprinkle parsley over cheese and serve.

Sunday Meatloaf for Six

4 pieces whole-wheat or white bread with crust
1 cup milk
2 eggs
1 pound ground round beef
1 pound ground pork
1 pound ground veal
1 teaspoon dried oregano
1 teaspoon dried thyme
2 large garlic cloves
¼ teaspoon cayenne pepper
1½ teaspoons salt
15 grinds fresh black pepper (approximately ½ teaspoon)
¾ cup ketchup
1½ cups (1 15-ounce can) tomato sauce
1 cup dark brown sugar
4 strips smoked bacon
½ cup water

Preheat oven to 350 degrees.

In a small bowl, soak bread in milk for up to 5 minutes or until most of milk is absorbed.

In a large mixing bowl, add eggs, meat, oregano, thyme, garlic, cayenne pepper, salt, pepper, ketchup, and soaked bread. Using your hands, blend and knead meat mixture for about a minute to be sure it is well-blended. Shape into a large ball.

In a medium-sized roasting pan, place meat in the center of pan and shape into a loaf or a football shape. The loaf should be wider in the middle and tapered at the ends.

Pour tomato sauce over the top of the meatloaf. Sprinkle brown sugar over top and sides of loaf.

Lay bacon strips lengthwise over meatloaf. Pour water around bottom of pan.

Bake for 50–60 minutes

Remove meatloaf from the oven and slice. Spoon out any fat in sauce. Spoon tomato sauce in pan over slices or serve in a gravy boat. Serve with buttered parsley noodles (recipe at right). A nice accompaniment to the noodles are peas and carrots (see recipe on next page).

Buttered Parsley Noodles

Buttered noodles go well with meat, stews, and meatloaf. The buttery noodles soak up all the robust flavors from the meat and make a perfect accompaniment as an alternative to mashed potatoes.

These noodles are a must in our family with stews and meatloaf!

1 teaspoon salt, divided
1 pound wide egg noodles (such as Pennsylvania Dutch brand)
½ stick salted butter, cut into 4 slices
¼ teaspoon freshly ground black pepper
8 sprigs flat parsley, leaves only, chopped finely

Fill a medium-sized stockpot ¾ with water. Add ½ teaspoon salt. Bring to a boil. Add noodles and cook until al dente, just before done. Noodles are done when they are chewy but still slightly firm, not soft. While noodles are cooking, put butter, ½ teaspoon salt, and ¼ teaspoon black pepper in a bowl.

Optional: Melt butter in a small pot before adding to bowl. Drain noodles when done.

Add hot noodles to bowl over the butter, salt, and pepper. Wait one minute before mixing to allow butter to melt. Mix with tongs or 2 forks. Taste for salt and pepper. Sprinkle with chopped parsley and mix gently. Serve.

Peas and Carrots

4 carrots, peeled and cut into 1-inch pieces
2 boxes frozen baby peas or fresh peas, if
    available. Note: If using fresh peas, add 5
    minutes to cooking time
2 tablespoons salted butter
Salt and pepper, to taste

Peel and cut carrots with a wave cutter or a knife on the diagonal. In a small saucepan, cover carrots with water and bring to a boil. Cook for 10 minutes or until carrots are soft but firm. Drain all but a ¼ cup of water. Add peas. Heat for 3 minutes (8 minutes if using fresh peas). Stir in butter. Salt and pepper to taste. Serve.

Old-Fashioned Banana Split

3 large bananas
½ gallon vanilla ice cream
1 cup maple syrup
2 cups good quality chocolate sauce (or use
    recipe below)
½ cup chopped peanuts or almonds
1 cup whipped cream (optional)
6 maraschino cherries (optional)

Slice one banana lengthwise and cut in half. Lay banana slices in a banana boat dish or in a small dessert bowl. Add 2 scoops of vanilla ice cream, drizzle with maple syrup and chocolate sauce. Sprinkle with chopped peanuts or almonds. Add whipped cream and maraschino cherries, if desired.

Chocolate Sauce

1½ cups milk, divided
12 ounces bittersweet chocolate, divided. A
    good chocolate with 60% plus cacao is
    recommended
1 cup sugar
2 teaspoons almond extract (optional)

In a saucepan over low heat, add 1 cup of milk and half the chocolate. When chocolate is melted, add the remaining chocolate and sugar. Stir and taste. Add a ½ cup more milk if too thick. If necessary, add an additional ¼ cup of sugar. Add almond extract, if desired. After the ingredients have dissolved, simmer for 7–10 minutes until sauce is thickened, stirring occasionally.

Can be made ahead and stored for several days. Reheat on low heat.

Spaghetti with Veal Meatball Dinner

serves 4

Avocado and Hearts of Palm Salad • Veal Meatballs and Spaghetti

Marinated Orange Sections in Grand Marnier

Many friends who have tried my veal meatballs describe them as moist and scrumptious. I have a little secret that helps to makes these meatballs unique. The type of bread used, along with the cooking method, truly help to make these veal meatballs delicious.

Avocado and hearts of palm are among my favorite vegetables. While at Bice restaurant recently, in Milan, I had a similar salad. This first course has a beautiful presentation and is a true palate pleaser.

Avocado and Hearts of Palm Salad

    Juice of one medium-sized lemon
    4 tablespoons extra virgin olive oil
    Salt, to taste
    12 grinds fresh black pepper (about ½ teaspoon)
    3 ripe avocados, sliced in ½-inch pieces
    1 can hearts of palm, sliced in ¼-inch rounds
    12 very thin slices Parmigiano Reggiano cheese

In a small bowl, blend lemon juice, olive oil, salt, and pepper.

On four individual salad plates, divide the slices of avocado and lay avocado slices in a circle. Now lay the hearts of palm slices in center of avocado circle.

Drizzle salad dressing over avocado and hearts of palm.

Lay 3 slices of cheese on top of hearts of palm and avocado. You may want to serve additional dressing on the side.

Serve immediately.

Veal Meatballs and Spaghetti
Serves 4 with additional for freezing for another meal

- 4 light whole-wheat hamburger buns (Arnold or Pepperidge Farm)
- 1½ cups milk
- 3 large eggs
- 3 pounds ground veal
- 4 teaspoons dried thyme
- 1 teaspoon oregano
- 5 tablespoons flat parsley, chopped
- 1½ teaspoons cayenne pepper (use less if you like it less spicy)
- 4 teaspoons salt
- Fresh ground pepper, about 40 grinds or 1½ teaspoons
- 9 medium-sized garlic cloves, pressed or minced
- 1½ cups Parmigiano Reggiano cheese, grated
- 2 tablespoons canola oil
- 4 tablespoons butter

Soak buns in milk for 5 minutes while you are preparing herbs and garlic.

In a large bowl, beat 3 eggs. Then add meat, herbs, garlic, and Parmigiano Reggiano. Use your hands to knead the meat. Squeeze some of milk from buns and add buns to meat. Blend with your knuckles, somewhat like a kneading motion, until all ingredients are blended together.

In a large skillet, heat canola oil and butter on medium-high heat.

At this point, start making your meatballs by rolling them between your palms until they are nice and round.

I prefer veal meatballs a medium-size, about 1¾–2" in diameter.

When butter and oil are bubbling, add your meatballs and brown on all sides, about 5 minutes. Remove meatballs. Repeat until all meatballs are done. You may want to add more butter, if necessary. It is important not to overcook them. This step is to brown the meatballs, not to cook them through.

A medium-brown color is good.

Remove to a large plate. Add more meatballs until all are cooked. Can be done one day in advance. Veal meatballs freeze well. I always make extra for another dinner.

Tomato sauce:

Make your tomato sauce ahead of time, either earlier the same day or a day before. Refrigerate if preparing the day before.

- ½ cup extra virgin olive oil (preferably from Tuscany)
- 8 cloves garlic, smashed
- 3 28-ounce cans imported peeled tomatoes
- 2 teaspoons thyme
- 1 tablespoon oregano
- Salt and pepper, to taste
- ½ teaspoon crushed red pepper flakes
- 1 large onion, peeled and whole
- 12 basil leaves, chopped

In a large pot, add extra virgin olive oil on medium-high heat. Add garlic. Cook for 2–3 minutes. (Garlic should still be white or only lightly browned.)

When the oil is hot and smoking, add tomatoes.

Stir in thyme, oregano, salt, pepper, and crushed red pepper. Add whole onion. Cook for 15 minutes on medium-high heat, stirring occasionally. Lower heat and simmer for 10 more minutes.

Add meatballs to heated sauce and cook for 10 minutes. Add basil leaves and adjust salt and pepper to taste.

Serve over pasta. Can substitute with spaghettini, which is slightly thinner than spaghetti. Of course, either one is good.

Marinated Orange Sections in Grand Marnier

A refreshing and welcomed dessert after a heavy meal.

    6 large navel oranges
    3 tablespoons sugar
    1 cup Grand Marnier

Peel oranges with a small, sharp knife, pith and skin removed. Slice rind (skin) of oranges into thin strips. Add strips to a small saucepan with 3 tablespoons of sugar. Cut 2 of the oranges in half and squeeze juice into saucepan. Heat on medium heat for 3–5 minutes and stir.

Set aside until ready to use.

Marinade:

Put oranges into a large bowl. Add Grand Marnier to bowl. Now add 4 large peeled oranges. Turn to coat all the oranges. Cover with plastic wrap and refrigerate for 4 hours, turning occasionally to coat oranges with marinade.

When ready to serve, use a small sharp knife and slice orange sections vertically, leaving membrane in tact. Lay orange sections on 4 plates in a circular pattern. Garnish with sweetened orange rinds.

From the Sea–Gerard Drive Fish Soup by Pierre Franey
serves 6
Boston Lettuce Salad with Mustard *Vinaigrette* • Gerard Drive Fish Soup by Pierre Franey
BAV's Herbed Stuffed French Bread • Autumn Plum Tart

The late Pierre Franey, world-renowned chef and food columnist, lived in East Hampton on Girard Drive for many years. He was also a noted cookbook author. He and his colleague Craig Claiborne, wrote the *New York Times 60 Minute Gourmet* cookbook, which has been my go-to book for many years. Pierre's wife, Betty, was kind enough to share her recipe with me for this cookbook many years ago.

Boston Lettuce Salad with Mustard *Vinaigrette*

During the summer months on the East End of Long Island, we can purchase fresh-picked lettuce daily at the farm stands. The tenderness of the just-picked lettuce is incredible and it makes this salad a delightful first course. I make an effort to buy organic whenever I can.

2 heads Boston lettuce, leaves washed and dried

Dressing:

6 tablespoons fine extra virgin olive oil
2 tablespoons red wine vinegar
2 teaspoons Dijon mustard, such as Grey Poupon
2 teaspoons each chopped fresh herbs: basil, thyme, and parsley (about 5 basil leaves, 3 sprigs of thyme, leaves only, and 4 stalks flat parsley, leaves only)
½ teaspoon salt
¼ teaspoon fresh ground pepper (6 grinds)

Optional: 1 small clove of garlic (or ½ large clove), minced or pressed.

Optional: ¼ cup cripy lardons, cubed, or any thick-cut bacon

Dressing can be made up to 4 days in advance.

In a dressing bottle or bowl blend all ingredients together. Shake or mix well with a spoon so oil, vinegar, and mustard form an emulsion.

Tear lettuce leaves in half or in thirds and place in a salad bowl. Pour half of the dressing on salad. With salad tongs or fork and spoon, gently toss. If more dressing is needed, add a little at a time. Taste for salt and pepper.

Serve immediately.

Gerard Drive Fish Soup

Recipe by Pierre Franey
Courtesy of Betty Franey

1¼ pound skinless tilefish, monkfish, or cod fillets
1 pound halibut or red snapper fillets
¼ cup olive oil
½ cups onion, finely chopped
1 cup celery, finely chopped
1 cup sweet green pepper, finely chopped
1 teaspoon fresh garlic, chopped
1 cup dry white wine
1 bay leaf
1 teaspoon dried thyme or 5 thyme sprigs
4 cups peeled crushed canned imported tomatoes
¼ teaspoon hot red pepper flakes
Salt and freshly ground black pepper, to taste
1 pound mussels, well-scrubbed and beards
   removed
½ pound shrimp, shelled and deveined
¼ cup fresh parsley leaves, chopped

Cut all the fish into 1½-inch cubes. Set them aside.

Heat the oil in a large saucepan over medium heat and add the onion, celery, green pepper, and garlic. Cook, stirring for 5 minutes. Add the wine, bay leaf, and thyme. Cook for one minute. Stir in the tomatoes, pepper flakes, salt, and pepper and simmer for 10 minutes.

Add the fish and mussels, stir and cook over high heat for about 3 minutes. Add the shrimp and parsley and simmer for 3 minutes more. Remove the bay leaf. Serve with herb-stuffed French bread.

BAV's Herbed Stuffed French Bread

1 large French *baguette*
2 teaspoons fresh thyme leaves, chopped
2 teaspoons fresh oregano leaves, chopped
½ teaspoon fresh rosemary, finely chopped
6 tablespoons salted butter, melted

Preheat oven to 375 degrees.

With a large bread knife, cut *baguette* on the diagonal a slice ¾ of the way to bottom of loaf. Do not cut all the way through. Repeat until the end of loaf. Each diagonal cut should be 2 inches apart.

In a small bowl, mix all other ingredients together.

With a pastry brush, brush herbed butter on both sides of the incisions. Repeat until all sides are brushed with herb butter.

Wrap loaf in aluminum foil. Can be made up to 6 hours ahead of time and refrigerated. Bake for 15–20 minutes. Serve hot.

Autumn Plum Tart

The first time I made this tart was during a family gathering last Autumn in Bridgehampton. Believe it or not, I purchased the plums from the local supermarket and they were large, sweet plums. Everyone loved the sweet and tart flavor emanating from the plums. I adore this tart, because it enhances all the natural flavor of the plums with very little sugar added.

> 9-inch tart pan
>
> 7 large sweet plums, cut into ½-inch slices
> 3 tablespoons sugar

Mix plums with sugar and set aside.

Glaze:

> 3 tablespoons seedless raspberry jam
> ¼ cup water
> 2 tablespoons sugar
> 2 tablespoons Grand Marnier liqueur

In a small saucepan, add all ingredients and heat for 2 minutes.

Tart Crust:

> 1¼ cup flour
> 1 stick chilled unsalted butter, cut into 6 slices
> 3 teaspoons light brown sugar
> 3 tablespoons cold water

Preheat oven to 350 degrees.

In a small mixing bowl, add flour and chilled butter pieces. With your fingers, break butter up and blend into flour, almost in a pinching motion. This step can also be done in an electric mixer with a dough hook.

When butter is broken down, add sugar and water and gently blend in. Do not overwork the dough. Form a flat ball and wrap in plastic wrap for 30 minutes or refrigerate for up to one day. Dough can be frozen for up to 3 months.

After 30 minutes, roll out on a medium-sized plastic or wooden board. Be sure the dough has a border ½ inch larger than the pan. Here is a tip for less shrinkage: Refrigerate again after rolling dough. Place on board in the refrigerator for 20 minutes. Now lay dough in pan and gently press dough down around bottom and top edges. Trim off top overhang.

Cut out a round of parchment paper to fit the bottom of pan. Place parchment in pan and cover with pie weights or 2 cups of uncooked rice or beans. Add glaze to top edges. Bake for 10–15 minutes or until edges are lightly brown. Remove from oven and cool for 10 minutes.

Glaze the bottom of tart dough and sides. Add a teaspoon of glaze to plum mixture. Lay plum slices side by side in half moon design all around the circumference and bake for 40 minutes. Turn heat up to 400 degrees for 5 minutes. Plums skin should be darker in color. Let cool.

Serve with a scoop of *crème fraîche* or vanilla ice cream.

Thursday Night Dinner
serves 4
Kristin's Guacamole and Chips • West Coast Chicken Tortilla Soup
Shrimp Tacos with Mango and Avocado Salsa • Margarita Cocktail • *Madeleines*

My husband and I would stay at the Hotel Bel-Air in Los Angeles annually. One of the treats of our trip would always be the best tortilla soup in one of the most beautiful garden settings. It is a destination lunch we always cherish. Since the Bel Air is under new ownership, the chicken tortilla soup has changed, and I prefer the original version from years ago.

It is a crowd pleaser with my guests when we pass around small bowls of fried tortillas, avocado, and cheese condiments to add to our soup. It makes a colorful and festive first course.

Kristin's Guacamole and Chips

Kristin with her Guacamole

2 medium-sized ripe tomatoes, seeded and cut in half
2 ripe avocados
Juice of 1 lime
½ jalapeno pepper, seeded, or more to your liking (Do not touch seeds when cutting the jalapeno pepper. Use rubber kitchen gloves and take care to wash hands after handling pepper, particularly the seeds.)
3 tablespoons fresh cilantro, chopped
4 tablespoons red onion, chopped (optional)
Salt, to taste

Seed tomatoes by cutting tomato in half; with a small spoon, take out the seeds. Squeeze juice from tomatoes and discard the juice. Coarsely chop tomatoes. Cut avocados in half and save one pit. Peel skin off (it is normally easy to peel) or scoop the avocado out of the skin with a tablespoon.

In a bowl, add lime juice and avocado and stir. Now add the tomatoes and remaining ingredients.

Mix gently, taking care not to mash the avocados. Serve with blue and white tortilla chips.

Important tip: Place avocado pit in middle of Guacamole in bowl. Along with lime juice, this helps to keep the avocado from turning brown.

West Coast Chicken Tortilla Soup

Below is my adaptation of this excellent and robust soup. Serve it for a lunch alone or for a first course for dinner.

20 corn tortillas, 6 inches in diameter, cut into ¼-inch strips (julienne crosswise)

In a deep skillet, heat 2 inches of canola oil or vegetable oil on medium-high heat. Add ⅓ of the tortilla chips in one layer. Do not overlap them. Fry until medium brown in color, about 1 minute. Remove with a slotted spoon to a large plate lined with paper towels to drain. Continue frying the rest of strips in the same manner.

Reserve half of the tortillas for garnish. You can keep the tortilla strips in an air-tight container. This step can be done a day before.

Soup:

2¼ tablespoons ground cumin
¾ teaspoon cayenne pepper
1½ tablespoons sweet paprika
1½ teaspoons ground coriander
2 bay leaves
¾ cup extra virgin olive oil
10 medium-large garlic cloves, finely chopped or crushed
3 cups onions, finely chopped
2½ teaspoons salt
6 tablespoons fresh cilantro, finely chopped, divided
6 cups tomatoes, chopped (or whole canned tomatoes, chopped)
9 cups chicken broth
1 pound boneless and skinless chicken breast, cut into ¼-inch slices (cut on the bias)

You can poach chicken in 1 cup water in frying pan. If you have a grill it is better to grill the whole chicken breast then cut into strips. I do this often in the summer months. Shortcut: Buy a cooked rotisserie chicken and use the breast meat without the skin.

Put first five ingredients into a small dish or cup.

In a large pot, heat olive oil on medium heat. When oil is almost smoking, add the remaining tortilla strips and the spices in the cup. Cook for about 2 minutes. Add garlic and onion and sauté for about 4–5 minutes. Add salt and 4 tablespoons fresh cilantro (saving the remainder for garnish).

Stir for one minute and then add tomatoes and chicken broth. Bring to a slight boil, then simmer for 1 hour. Remove bay leaves and let cool for about 10 minutes.

In a blender or food processor, add soup in batches to purée. Strain through a fine sieve. Using the sieve is not a necessary step. I usually omit this for my family for a more rustic soup. For guests, using the sieve makes a more elegant soup with a silkier texture.

The soup can be made a day ahead and refrigerated.

Serving soup:

2 large ripe avocadoes, peeled and cut into ¼-inch chunks
1 cup extra-sharp cheddar cheese, shredded
1 cup aged Monterrey Jack cheese

Heat the soup over a low–medium heat. Add the chicken and the remaining cilantro. Cook over low heat for a few minutes more. Do not boil. Ladle into soup-bowls, making sure that each bowl has several pieces of chicken. Divide avocado pieces and place on top of soup (about 3 or 4 avocado pieces to each soup bowl).

Pass around the cheese and tortilla strips. Invite your guests to ladle a tablespoon of cheese and sprinkle several tortilla strips on their soup.

For my family, I just garnish the soup bowls with the cheese and tortilla strips in the kitchen.

Shrimp Tacos with Mango and Avocado Salsa

Shrimp tacos are great for lunch or dinner. It is a festive meal and also great for a weekend meal. I like to offer everyone a Margarita cocktail with guacamole and tortilla chips.

Shrimp:

> 1½ pounds large shrimp, shelled and cleaned (can substitute 4 cod fillets or any white flaky fish)
> 4 garlic cloves, crushed
> 3 tablespoons extra virgin olive oil
> ¼ teaspoon sea salt
> ½ teaspoon freshly ground pepper
> Juice of 2 limes
> 5 or 6 skewers
> 2 tablespoons canola oil (if using grill pan or sauté pan)

In a bowl or deep plate, mix shrimp with garlic, olive oil, salt, pepper, and half of the lime juice. Let marinate for 30 minutes. Skewer shrimp. Brush with marinade. Pour the rest of the lime juice on shrimp.

If you do not have an indoor or outdoor grill, grill pans are great for seafood or meats for use on the stovetop. A sauté pan can also be used.

Grill:

Heat the grill. When hot, grill skewered shrimp for about four minutes on each side. Brush with marinade while cooking to keep shrimp from drying out.

It is best to check one shrimp to see if it is cooked through. If it is opaque when you cut into center, cook for another 2 minutes.

Mango and avocado salsa:

>   1 ripe mango, chopped
>   1 ripe but firm avocado, coarsely chopped
>   1½ tablespoon extra virgin olive oil
>   Juice of 2 limes
>   ½ red onion, finely chopped
>   5 tablespoons fresh cilantro, chopped
>   ⅛ teaspoon cayenne pepper (less if you do not
>   like it spicy)
>   Sea salt, to taste

Prepare salsa by mixing all ingredients together. Salsa can be made several hours earlier and kept in an airtight container until ready to use.

Whole-wheat tortillas:

>   4 10-inch whole-wheat flour soft tortillas

To heat the whole-wheat tortillas, roll several in a paper towel and place in microwave oven for 40 seconds. Repeat for extras.

Fill each tortilla with shrimp and top with salsa. Now wrap it (turn in bottom and fold both sides over each other). Serve with a wedge of lime.

Margarita Cocktail

>   8 ounces good quality 100% Agave tequila
>   2 ounces fresh lime juice
>   2 ounces fresh lemon juice
>   4 ounces triple sec or Grand Marnier
>
>   fine sea salt for the glass rims
>   1 lime sliced in ¼-inch rounds for glasses

Mix tequila, lime juice, lemon juice, and triple sec in a cocktail shaker filled with ice. Moisten the rim of the cocktail glass with a slice of lime. Place the sea salt in a small flat dish. Dip the rim of the cocktail glass in the salt until lightly coated. Shake all ingredients, strain and serve.

Madeleines

Makes 16

>   *Madeleine* pan with 16 molds
>
>   3 eggs
>   ⅓ cup sugar
>   Pinch of salt
>   2 cups all-purpose flour
>   1½ teaspoons baking powder
>   1 navel orange, zest only (about 1 tablespoon or
>   more)
>   ⅔ cup unsalted butter, melted
>   3 tablespoons softened butter for buttering pan
>   (Butter can be microwaved. Cover bowl with
>   a plate or plastic wrap and microwave for 30
>   seconds.)
>   3 tablespoons confectioners' sugar

Preheat oven to 425 degrees.

In a mixing bowl, combine eggs, sugar, and salt. Using a whisk or electric mixer, cream eggs until pale yellow, about 4 minutes. Should be thick and fluffy. Slowly beat in flour and baking powder until blended. Stir in orange zest. Using a rubber spatula, gently fold in half the melted butter, then fold in the rest. To ensure fluffy and light *Madeleines*, do not mix, just fold in butter to lightly blend.

With a pastry brush, butter *Madeleine* molds in pan, being sure to get into the ridges. Place a heaping 1 tablespoon of batter into each mold.

Bake for 8–12 minutes until tops of *Madeleines* spring back when touched.

Remove from oven and invert pan on a wire rack. Gently tap back of molds and *Madeleines* should release. If they are stuck, then use your fingers to loosen the edges, being careful of the hot pan. Allow to cool on the rack.

Place confectioners' sugar in a small sieve and shake over each *Madeleine,* dusting the tops.

On dessert plates, serve 4 per person. Can be served with sorbet or ice cream.

New Orleans-Style Barbecue Shrimp Lunch

serves 4

Tomato, Cucumber, and Mint Salad • New Orleans-Style Barbecue Shrimp
Caramelized Banana Walnut Tart with Almond Butter

The first time I tasted this mouth-watering shrimp dish was at Pascal's Manale Restaurant, a family-owned-and-operated landmark in New Orleans since 1913. New Orleans is renowned for the finest Cajun cuisine. Visiting New Orleans is a gastronome's delight! With a loaf of crusty French bread and our hands covered with buttery sauce, my husband and I licked our bowls clean. In the authentic preparation, they cook the prawns in their shells, which fortifies the shrimp flavor.

For those who dislike dipping their fingers in the sauce, it is best to shell the shrimp before cooking. I cook it both ways. It depends whether you are serving them as a first course or as casual meal with friends or family as an entrée, where I leave the shells on.

Everyone invited was asked to bring a dish to share to a *Viva la France* theme party at Michael and Christine Aaron's home (Michael was then a partner in Sherry Lehman Wines). It was the highlight of the night when Pierre Franey tasted my New Orleans-style barbecue shrimp and raved about them. Pierre said, "*C'est vraiment magnifique!*"

Tomato, Cucumber, and Mint Salad

I had this salad for the first time was when I was a small girl traveling with my parents through Spain. My mother bought cucumbers and tomatoes from a roadside stand and we stopped at a nearby café to have something to drink. The owner told my mother to give her the tomatoes and cucumbers and she would prepare them for her. That benevolent woman took them into the kitchen and came out 5 minutes later with this wonderful, refreshing salad. This is my adaptation of that special tomato, cucumber, and mint salad that has been indelibly imprinted in my memory all of these years!

4 large ripe tomatoes, cut into 2-inch wedges
6 Kirby or Persian cucumbers, cut into ¾-inch slices
12 fresh mint leaves, sliced into strips
3 tablespoons extra virgin olive oil
2 tablespoons red wine vinegar
½ teaspoon salt
½ teaspoon freshly ground pepper

On an oval or round serving platter, add tomatoes, cucumbers, and mint. In a small bowl, mix together oil, vinegar, salt, and pepper; pour over tomatoes and cucumbers. Mix with a fork and spoon so dressing is distributed evenly. Taste for salt and pepper. Add an extra tablespoon of oil and vinegar, if necessary. Let sit for up to 30 minutes before serving, allowing the tomatoes to absorb some of the dressing. This salad is one of my favorite summer salads. It's so fresh you can taste summer.

New Orleans-Style Barbecue Shrimp

3 sticks salted butter
8 large cloves garlic, finely chopped
1 teaspoon black pepper, freshly ground
½ teaspoon crushed hot red pepper flakes
1 teaspoon thyme
1 teaspoon oregano
½ teaspoon marjoram
¼ teaspoon white pepper
16 jumbo shrimp in their shell
½ cup shrimp stock (see recipe at right)
½ cup white wine
2 tablespoons Worcestershire sauce

In a large frying pan, large enough to accommodate all the shrimp in one layer, melt butter on medium-high heat. When melted, add garlic. Heat until light brown and add spices (next six ingredients). Stir and add shrimp. If necessary, use another pan and split sauce and shrimp. Shrimp should not be overlapped.

Cook shrimp for 3 minutes. Turn shrimp over and add shrimp stock, wine, and Worcestershire sauce. Stir well. Cook for about 10 minutes until shrimp are cooked through. Stir occasionally.

Jumbo shrimp take longer than large shrimp. Adjust cooking time and always check by cutting into one shrimp, making sure it is cooked through.

Serve shrimp with a generous portion of sauce in shallow bowls. Best served with crusty warm French bread.

Simple shrimp stock:

Shrimp stock can be frozen for up to 3 months.

3 cups water
About 2 dozen shrimp shells
1 small onion, whole, peeled
6 peppercorns
1 teaspoon sea salt
½ bunch flat parsley

Ask your fishmonger or supermarket for about 2 dozen shrimp shells. Add all ingredients to a soup pot. Bring to a boil. Then simmer for 2 hours or more until you have about a cup of broth left. Strain the stock.

The shrimp stock can be made a day in advance, tightly covered, and refrigerated or frozen. I often freeze some of the shrimp stock in ½ cup freezer containers, so I have it on hand for future use.

Caramelized Banana Walnut Tart with Almond Butter

Serves 8–10

A few of my favorite things are almond butter, walnuts, and bananas. I always keep almond butter in my pantry. It is full of antioxidants. Walnuts are a great source of Omega 3 and bananas are full of potassium.

The flavorful combination makes this tart a dessert winner. Seconds are very common when I serve this savory tart!

One 10-inch tart pan

One *Pâte Brisée* recipe for tart crust (see page 45). Make at least one hour ahead

- ¾ cup granulated sugar
- ½ cup almond milk
- ¾ cup heavy cream
- 1½ cups walnuts, chopped
- ¼ cup almond butter (can be purchased at most markets and heath food stores)
- 5 large ripe bananas, cut into ½-inch slices

Preheat oven to 375 degrees.

Over medium-high heat, add sugar to a medium-sized saucepan. Stir with a wooden spoon until sugar melts and caramelizes, about 8 minutes. It will turn a medium brown. Keep stirring, scraping sides of pot as you stir. Immediately add almond milk, cream, and chopped walnuts. Take caution that the milk mixture when added to the hot caramel does not splatter. When added, the liquid caramel will turn hard like candy. Continue stirring until it melts into the milk mixture. Remove from heat.

Roll out tart dough and fit into a 10-inch tart pan. Press dough to the sides of pan to help prevent shrinkage. Prick several holes in bottom of dough. Refrigerate for 10 minutes. Remove from refrigerator and evenly spread almond butter with a spoon or flat metal spatula on bottom of tart dough.

Layer 4 bananas in circular rows around tart pan leaving no gaps. If necessary, add another banana. Pour milk mixture over bananas and bake for 45–50 minutes.

Remove from oven. Cool for 5 minutes. It may be necessary to take a thin, flat knife and carefully separate the side crust from the tart pan before pushing the bottom of pan up to unmold tart.

Can be made one day in advance. When ready to serve, reheat for 5–8 minutes in a 350-degree oven. Make sure not to overcook.

Serve with whipped cream or vanilla ice cream.

Autumn Saturday Dinner for Eight

serves 8

Queensland Blue Pumpkin Soup with *Crème Fraîche* • Rib Pork Chops with *Gorgonzola Dolce* and Figs
Peas and Pearl Onions • Fingerling Potatoes • Gingersnap Cake with Lemon Cream

A dinner made in heaven for pork lovers. It is a unique dinner to serve friends on a Saturday night. The pork is moist and tender when cooked properly and the sweet Gorgonzola and figs add a burst of flavor to the pork.

Queensland Blue Pumpkin Soup with *Crème Fraîche*

Autumn is one of my favorite seasons. The farm stands are full of all varieties of squash and pumpkins. Every few years I ask the farmers "Which pumpkin is best for soup?" Most of them say the cheese pumpkin, which is flesh color. This year I asked Harry Ludlow of Fairview Farms, in Bridgehampton. They have a corn maze and pumpkin patch for families that is very popular on weekends in the fall. Harry said his wife, Barbara, has tried all the different varieties of pumpkins and she prefers the sweetness of the Queensland Blue pumpkin or the Hubbard, a long green weird-shaped pumpkin. I agree with Barbara. The Queensland Blue pumpkin's deep orange flesh is sweet and full of flavor. You can be the judge.

 1 large Queensland Blue pumpkin, about 6–7 cups (or 2 small to medium-sized pumpkins)
 6 cups chicken broth, divided
 ¼ teaspoon allspice
 1 teaspoon nutmeg (freshly grated preferred)
 1¼ cups half-and-half
 2 teaspoons salt
 White pepper, freshly ground preferred, to taste
 ¾ cup *crème fraîche* (optional)
 8 stalks chives, cut in quarters

Preheat oven to 375 degrees.

Cut pumpkin in half and spoon out seeds and threads. An Ice cream scoop is a good tool for scooping out the seeds. Place pumpkin halves on a cookie sheet and roast for 60 minutes or until flesh is tender and soft. Remove from oven and scoop out all the tender flesh and discard skin.

Blend pumpkin in food processor for 1 minute until puréed and smooth.

In a medium-sized stockpot, add pumpkin purée, 3 cups of chicken broth, allspice, and nutmeg. Stir until blended and let thicken. Add a little more chicken broth until soup has a silky consistency. Cook for 5 minutes and add the half-and-half. Taste for salt and pepper. Ladle into bowls; add a teaspoon of *crème fraîche* and garnish with chives.

Rib Pork Chops with *Gorgonzola Dolce* and Figs

 8 rib pork chops, 1¼ –1½ inches thick

Ask your butcher to cut a 1-inch pocket in each chop. You can also cut the pocket yourself. Make sure you do not make opening too wide. It is okay to make a wider pocket on inside to stuff the pocket with enough *Gorgonzola Dolce* cheese.

 12-ounce wedge sweet Gorgonzola cheese (also known as *Gorgonzola Dolce*)

Break up into 8 pieces, about 1½ tablespoons each.

Wooden toothpicks: Soak toothpicks for a few minutes in a small bowl of water. This prevents them from burning.

 1 teaspoon dried thyme
 1 teaspoon dried oregano
 3 tablespoons olive oil
 Non-stick cooking spray

Preheat oven to 425 degrees.

Mix thyme and oregano together. Rub oil on both sides of pork chops. Then rub dried herbs on both sides.

Stuff each chop with cheese and secure opening of pocket with 3 or 4 toothpicks.

Coat bottom of a large grill pan or grill with non-stick cooking spray. When pan is hot, add pork chops in batches. Sear for 4 minutes on each side. Remove and put chops in a large roasting pan and roast in oven for 10 minutes.

Pork can be slightly pink when done. If you overcook pork, it can become dry.

Note: During the summer, I prefer to grill these chops on my outdoor grill for 3 minutes on each side and then roast in the oven for 10 minutes.

Figs:

  2 tablespoons butter
  16 ripe figs, cut in half lengthwise
  5 tablespoons balsamic vinegar

In a medium-sized sauté pan, melt butter. Add figs and balsamic vinegar. Stir. Cook for 5 minutes until sauce thickens slightly.

Spoon 4 fig halves per person with balsamic sauce next to each pork chop.

Peas and Pearl Onions

  ½ cup water
  2 boxes good quality frozen peas (Fresh peas are preferred but may be hard to find year round)
  2 dozen pearl onions (Tip: To make peeling the pearl onions easier, I place them in a small pot of boiling water for 2 minutes. Drain and when slightly cooled, peel the onions.)
  1 tablespoon butter
  Salt and pepper, to taste

In a medium-sized saucepan, add water, peas, and onions. Bring to a boil. Stir and cook for 3 minutes until peas are firm, not mushy. Remove from heat. Add butter, salt, and pepper to taste. Mix and serve.

Fingerling Potatoes

Fingerling potatoes are small in size and are shaped like a finger. They are very popular and contain a rich and nutty flavor. Russian bananas, a yellow-skinned variety of fingerling potatoes, are seen mostly at farm stands in the Bridgehampton area. Simply roast them in the oven for 20–25 minutes and have a delicious side with a meat, fish, or poultry dish.

  16 fingerling potatoes
  ¼ cup extra virgin olive oil
  2 garlic cloves, pressed
  2 teaspoons coarse sea salt
  ¼ teaspoon freshly ground pepper
  2 sprigs rosemary, leaves chopped

Preheat oven to 375 degrees.

On a baking sheet, add potatoes, olive oil, garlic, salt, pepper, and chopped rosemary. With a spoon or hands, roll potatoes so they are coated well with olive oil, garlic, and rosemary. If you need more olive add an extra tablespoon.

Roast for 20–25 minutes. Serve.

Gingersnap Cake with Lemon Cream

Recipe contributed by Lauren Torrisi

Cake:

- 1¼ cups all-purpose flour
- 2 teaspoons baking powder
- ½ teaspoon coarse salt (Kosher salt or sea salt)
- ½ teaspoon cinnamon
- ¼ teaspoon ground cloves
- 2 teaspoons ground ginger
- ¼ cup brown sugar, packed
- ½ cup white sugar
- ½ cup canola oil
- 2 tablespoons molasses
- 1 teaspoon pure vanilla extract
- 2 large eggs, room temperature
- ¼ cup buttermilk, room temperature

Preheat oven to 350 degrees.

In a medium bowl, mix together flour, baking powder, salt, cinnamon, ground cloves, and ginger. Set aside.

In the bowl of a stand mixer or electric hand mixer, whisk together brown and white sugars to remove any clumps.

Add oil and whisk for 1–2 minutes on medium speed. Add molasses.

Add vanilla and eggs, whisking 5 minutes on medium-high speed.

Alternate adding buttermilk and flour mixture, starting with the flour. Do not overmix.

Pour into an 8-inch greased cake pan. Bake for 20–25 minutes, until a toothpick comes out clean. Let cool completely.

Blackberries:

- 2 pints (1 pint chopped blackberries for filling, 1 pint whole berries for garnish)

Lemon cream filling:

- 1½ cups whipping cream
- 3 tablespoons confectioners' sugar
- ½ cup lemon curd (can be purchased in most supermarkets in the jam and preserves section)

Whip the cream to soft peaks. Fold in the confectioners' sugar and lemon curd.

*Note: Some store-bought lemon curd can be too thick. Mix 1 tablespoon cream with the curd before adding it to the rest of the cream to avoid getting lumps.

To assemble:

Once cake is cooled, cut in half horizontally. Spread a thin layer of blackberries on the bottom layer. Spread 1 cup of the filling over the berries. Put the top layer of cake over the berries. Ice the cake with the remainder of the lemon frosting. Top with fresh blackberries and mint sprigs.

Photo by Lauren Torrisi

Pre-Thanksgiving Dinner
serves 6 to 8
Tomato, Red Onion, Basil with Balsamic *Vinaigrette* • Lobster and Shrimp *Fra Diavolo*
Poached Pears with *Gorgonzola Dolce*

One of our favorite family gatherings is having Thanksgiving in our home in Bridgehampton. Generally family and guests arrive the day before this special day of thanks. By that time, the blazingly colorful leaves of autumn have virtually disappeared from the trees and there is a chill in the air. Everyone gathers around the fireplace and our holiday begins. We have a ritual that we have been doing for years. Our pre-Thanksgiving dinner is Lobster and Shrimp *Fra Diavolo* with Linguine.

Tomato, Red Onion, Basil with Balsamic *Vinaigrette*

4 ¼-inch slices red onion
3 large ripe hot-house tomatoes or any large ripe tomatoes, sliced into 4 pieces
12 medium-sized fresh basil leaves

Soak red onion slices in a bowl of cold water for 15 minutes change water once after 5 minutes. This takes the bitterness from the onions.

On 6 individual plates, place one slice of tomato on each plate, 2 leaves of basil on top, then onion, tomato slice, and one basil leaf on top.

Dressing:

8 tablespoons extra virgin olive oil
6 tablespoons balsamic vinegar
½ teaspoon sugar
3 teaspoons white wine mustard

Whisk ingredients together until it is smooth and creamy in texture.

Add about 2 tablespoons on top of tomatoes and serve.

Note: A fine, aged balsamic vinegar enhances the flavor of this lovely first course.

Lobster and Shrimp *Fra Diavolo*

You can ask the fish department in your local market to prepare the lobsters and crack the claws to make them easier to eat. The tails should be split in half and detached from the body as well as the claws.

Alternatively, you can crack the claws yourself with a mallet or small hammer. Tip: Lay a clean dish cloth over the claws when cracking with a hammer to keep juices from spraying all over.

4 tablespoons extra virgin olive oil, divided
8 cloves garlic, sliced thinly, divided
6 lobsters, claws and tails only
2 dozen large shrimp, uncooked and cleaned, shells removed
3 28-ounce cans imported Italian crushed tomatoes
1 tablespoon dried thyme or 2 tablespoons fresh thyme
1 teaspoon dried oregano
1½ teaspoons salt
1 teaspoon cayenne pepper (for less spicy, add ½ teaspoon)
4 stalks fresh flat parsley, leaves only, finely chopped (for garnish)

Lobster:

You can ask the fishmonger to cut the tails and claws for you. However, you want to cook them as soon as possible. Lobster should be refrigerated or cooked the same day they are purchased.

In a large deep skillet on medium-high heat, add 2 tablespoons olive oil.

Add 2 cloves of garlic slices. Heat for 1 minute then, add lobster tails and claws. Stir and cook for 3–4 minutes until they turn red. Remove from pan. Add remainder of oil and turn heat to high. Add shrimp. Sear on one side for 2 minutes and turn over and sear for another 2 minutes. Remove shrimp.

When oil is hot again, add the remainder of the garlic. After about a minute, add tomatoes, thyme, and oregano. Stir and cook for 10 minutes on medium heat. Add salt and cayenne pepper. Stir occasionally. Add back lobster and shrimp and cook on medium-low heat for 8–10 minutes.

Fill a large pot ¾ with water and bring to a boil. Add salt after water is boiling, then add linguini. Cook until al dente. Drain. Using kitchen tongs, put equal portions of linguini in pasta bowls or plates. Spoon tomato sauce over pasta with equal portions of lobster and shrimp per serving. Sprinkle with chopped parsley and serve.

Note: When preparing the tomato sauce a ahead of time (can be made several days prior), omit lobster and refrigerate sauce.

When ready, heat lobster in a medium-sized pot with 2 tablespoons olive oil until it turns red, about 4–5 minutes. Add tomato sauce and cook for 10–15 minutes. Prepare pasta as above.

Poached Pears with *Gorgonzola Dolce*

Gorgonzola Dolce's texture is very soft and sweeter than regular Gorgonzola. It can be found in many supermarkets, specialty gourmet markets, and Italian markets.

Wine, pears, and *Gorgonzola Dolce* make a winning combination and I love this dessert. It is perfect following a substantial dinner and great for parties because it can be prepared days in advance. I often serve it during the Christmas holiday season.

It is also wonderful in the late summer and early autumn when the pears are just picked from our trees in Bridgehampton. Buy them hard and after 1 or 2 days poach them or wait another day and eat them fresh.

6 Bosc pears (or any firm-flesh pear)
1 bottle (4 cups) red table wine
1 6-inch sprig fresh rosemary
4 branches fresh thyme
6 whole cloves
2 tablespoons sugar
1 cinnamon stick (can substitute 1 teaspoon ground cinnamon)
12 ounces *Gorgonzola Dolce*

Note: It is important to use a harder pear for poaching. The Bosc pears are perfect for poaching and their graceful stance makes for a lovely presentation.

Using a vegetable or carrot peeler, peel pears, taking care to leave the stem on top of each pear. Carefully peel any skin around the stem.

Add pears, wine, and all other ingredients except cheese to a stockpot. Bring to a boil and lower to medium-low heat and cook for 10 minutes. With a spoon, gently turn pears over so that all sides are cooking evenly in wine. Cook for another 10 minutes until pears are still slightly firm but tender. Test with the point of a small sharp knife by poking gently into the middle of a pear.

Remove from heat and let sit in wine until cool. Cover pears until ready to use. Can be made up to 3 days in advance and refrigerated in an airtight container.

Serve each pear standing up on a dessert plate. Drizzle some of the glaze around the pear or spoon a generous tablespoon in the center of dessert plate and place pear on top. Now scoop a few chunks of the *Gorgonzola Dolce* next to each pear.

Thanksgiving Dinner with Free-Range Turkey

serves 12

Shrimp *Bisque* • Roast Turkey • Spiced Sausage Nut Stuffing • Cranberry Chutney with Mango
Fennel *Au Gratin* • Brussels Sprouts with *Pancetta* • Baked Glazed Yams with Pecans
Spiced Pumpkin Pie with Whipped Cream

Thanksgiving always comes upon us faster than we anticipate . . . and the turkey farmers at Ludlow's and North Sea Farms make sure they have enough turkeys for their loyal customers. Believe it or not, September is the time to order a turkey for Thanksgiving from Art Ludlow in Bridgehampton.

He and his brother, Harry, also make fabulous breakfast sausage, which can only be ordered with your turkey for Thanksgiving. Also around Thanksgiving, I am always one of the first to order Harry's homemade spicy sausage. It is an excellent addition to my turkey stuffing.

Shrimp *Bisque*

For the stock:

3 tablespoons butter
2½ pounds medium shrimp with shells, head (if possible), and tails
2 medium-sized carrots, chopped
1 small onion, chopped, or ½ large onion
2 stalks celery, chopped
3 large garlic cloves, pressed or chopped
4 sprigs thyme
9 cups water
4 cups fish broth
1 *bouquet garni*: 4 sprigs parsley, 2 sprigs rosemary, and 2 thyme and/or dill (herbs tied with a clean string or in cheesecloth for easy removal)
¼ teaspoon salt

For the soup:

2 medium-sized ripe tomatoes, cut into quarters
6 tablespoons butter, divided
1½ cups white wine
½ teaspoon sea salt (taste for extra)
¼ teaspoon cayenne pepper
12 grinds fresh white pepper (½ teaspoon ground white pepper)
½ cup white flour
2 tablespoons tomato paste
¼ cup cognac
1¼ cups heavy cream

Remove shells of 12 shrimp and de-vein. Set aside and refrigerate until ready to use.

To make the stock, melt the butter in a large pot. Add remaining shrimp in shells to stockpot. Stir shrimp for one minute. Add carrots, onion, celery, garlic, and thyme. Stir for another minute. Now add water, fish broth, *bouquet garni*, and salt. Bring to a boil. Cook for 1 hour on low heat, uncovered. Strain broth and set aside. Reserve shrimp and vegetables.

In a food processor, pulse the quartered tomatoes and shrimp in their shells, several pulses. Yes, you read that correctly. Most of the flavor is in the shell. Most chefs know that shrimp is most flavorful when cooked in its shell.

Place a medium-sized sieve over a mixing bowl. Add reserved vegetables from stock along with puréed shrimp and tomato mixture to sieve.

This step is well worth the 3 minutes it takes to press all the flavorful liquid from the shrimp and vegetables. Use a heavy wooden spoon or a potato masher to press liquid from vegetables. Do this until there is no more liquid coming through the sieve. Every drop is important. The pressed vegetable broth that you now have is what makes this delectable soup a hit. It should be at least a cup or more.

In a large saucepan, melt a tablespoon of butter. Turn heat up to medium-high and add 12 cleaned shrimp. When lightly brown on each side (about 2 minutes on each side), add wine. Stir the brown bits in the pan and blend into the wine. Let wine boil and reduce. After

2 minutes, add shrimp stock, the pressed vegetable broth, salt, cayenne pepper, and white pepper. Stir. Lower heat to simmer.

In a small bowl, mix flour with 5 tablespoons room-temperature butter. Mash together with a fork or use your fingers. When blended together (almost dough-like), add about a ½ cup of soup to bowl and blend flour/butter mixture into liquid. This step makes it easier for the flour not to lump in the soup. Add to soup. Stir, over medium heat and add tomato paste, then cognac. Heat for another 2 minutes. Pour in 1 cup cream, a little at a time. Stir. Add an additional ¼ cup cream, if desired. Taste for salt. Add more white pepper, if needed.

Texture should be silky and smooth. Not too thin and not too thick. If soup is watery, reduce liquid by cooking on low heat until soup thickens. If soup is too thick, add more fish broth. This soup does not have a thick consistency like some traditional *bisques*.

Cut each whole shrimp in half and serve one shrimp per person in shallow-rimmed soup bowls. Rimmed bowls are preferable for serving shrimp bisque. Ladle approximately ¾ cup *bisque* over shrimp. Garnish with dill or any herb you have in the kitchen.

Roast Turkey

> 25-pound turkey (Cooking time - 7 hours. I usually figure 15 minutes per pound with stuffing. Fresh-killed turkeys tend to cook faster.)
> 1 orange, cut in half
> Salt and pepper
> 3 tablespoons butter
> 2 cups chicken broth
> Cheesecloth or thin dishcloth

Preheat oven to 400 degrees.

Wash the turkey well. Rinse with cold water inside the cavity until it runs clear.

Squeeze and rub orange halves all over the body of the turkey.

Put salt and pepper inside the cavity as well as the outside.

Stuff cavity and backside of turkey with dressing (see recipe on page 107) and truss the legs with kitchen string. Place turkey in a large roasting pan. Cut butter into slices and rub butter on the thigh joint areas and on top of the turkey. Roast turkey in the oven for 20 minutes. Then turn down the heat to 325 degrees.

Heat chicken broth in a medium-sized saucepan. Simmer. Use a turkey baster to baste the turkey. This is important, particularly in the beginning. I also dip the cheesecloth in the pot of broth and lay it on top of the turkey breast to keep it moist in between basting times.

Baste turkey every 20-30 minutes. Use baster to baste the cheesecloth and rest of turkey with broth. After several hours, there will probably be an accumulation of broth in the roasting pan. Use these pan juices as much as possible for basting now for the best flavor.

Dip cheesecloth in broth about 4 times during the roasting process.

Remove cheesecloth from the turkey 30–40 minutes before it is done. This will allow turkey breast to brown more.

Turkey is done when your poultry thermometer reads 180 degrees. Take out of oven and let rest for 35–40 minutes before carving.

Nick Verbitsky carving the Thanksgiving turkey

Spiced Sausage Nut Stuffing

Whenever I make this stuffing, I think of my dear friends Kari and Dick Clark. Dick said that this was his favorite stuffing and Kari makes it at least 3 times a year. This is a note from Kari:

> *Dear Bonnie,*
>
> *Made Thanksgiving dinner last night for an early 'Dick birthday dinner' with the kids. That was his request... his favorite dinner. His son and family (grandkids) were in from England. Just wanted to tell you that I made your dressing (stuffing) again and it was DELICIOUS! Everyone agreed. They hadn't had it before and were most impressed. There's nothing like it and I really appreciate your trouble in getting it to me last year.*
>
> *Love, Kari*

This recipe is enough for a 15–25 pound turkey with some left over.

- 1½–2 pounds ground spiced pork sausage
- 6 tablespoons butter
- 1 cup celery, finely chopped
- 1 cup carrots, finely chopped
- 1½ cups onions, chopped
- 2 tablespoons poultry seasoning
- 1 tablespoon dried thyme
- 1 teaspoon dried marjoram or dried oregano
- 1 tablespoon salt
- 2 teaspoons freshly ground pepper
- ½ teaspoon cayenne pepper
- 3½ cups chicken broth
- 1 large bag Pepperidge Farm Seasoned Bread Stuffing
- ½ large bag Pepperidge Farm Fancy Mixed Stuffing (The bread pieces are a little bigger, which add body to the smaller seasoned bread pieces)
- 1 cup whole roasted almonds
- 2 cups whole peeled chestnuts, cut in half
- 1 cup pecans

Note: It is not necessary to use the selection of almonds, chestnuts, and pecans in the stuffing mixture. Choose 2 types of nuts, if you prefer.

In a frying pan over medium-high heat, brown sausage until it is almost red in color, about 7–10 minutes.

In a large skillet, melt butter over medium heat. Mix in vegetables and seasonings.

Cook for 3–4 minutes until vegetables soften.

Add broth and bring to a boil. Remove from heat and add stuffing and nuts, stirring lightly with a fork to blend. When liquid has been absorbed, add sausage and mix.

Salt and pepper to taste.

Stuff both ends of your turkey. Do not pack stuffing in tightly. If you have more stuffing than the turkey can hold, bake it in a casserole dish for 20 minutes.

Tip: Sprinkle some chicken broth over the top of the casserole to keep stuffing slightly moist.

Freeze leftover stuffing . . . great with a roast chicken.

Peter Ludlow and Bonnie

Cranberry Chutney with Mango

This tangy chutney is a favorite at holiday time, and there are raves about this unique cranberry delight. Of course, there are always a few family holdouts who must have the traditional jellied cranberries from a can! I always serve both.

Spoon this wonderful Cranberry Chutney with Mango in a clear crystal bowl and garnish with kumquats and at Christmas, garnish with curly parsley around the perimeter.

½ teaspoon cloves
¼ teaspoon allspice
½ teaspoon curry powder
1 teaspoon ground cinnamon or 2 cinnamon sticks
½ cup cider vinegar
3 ¼-inch slices fresh ginger, peeled, smashed, and finely chopped.
2 cups light brown sugar
1¾ cups water
3 navel orange peels, grated, and orange sections
2 lemon peels, grated, and lemon sections
1 Granny Smith apple (or any tart apple), peeled, cored, and coarsely chopped
6 cups fresh cranberries, divided
¾ cup golden raisins
½ cup firm mango, cut into ¼-inch chunks
¾ cup chopped pecans

In a large saucepan, combine spices, vinegar, ginger, sugar, water, and grated rinds. Bring to a boil, stir until sugar is dissolved, and add lemon and orange sections and chopped apple. Reduce the heat to low and cook for 8–10 minutes.

At this point, add the cranberries at different intervals. This prevents all the cranberries from cooking at the same time. By adding the cranberries at intervals, some cranberries will be cooked through and soft and others will be whole, yet cooked.

Add 3 cups of cranberries and raisins. Lower heat to simmer and cook for 30 minutes more until mixture thickens. Then add 2 cups of cranberries and simmer for another 10 minutes.

Finish by adding the last cup of cranberries, chopped mango, and pecans. Simmer for 15 minutes. Remove from heat.

Pour cranberry compote into an airtight bowl. Let cool and refrigerate until ready to use. Can be refrigerated for 2 weeks or more if tighly covered. Great with leftover turkey and as an accompaniment to roast chicken.

Fennel *au Gratin*

3 large bulbs fennel
1½ cups heavy cream
½ teaspoon salt
½ teaspoon ground white pepper (black pepper can be substituted)
½ cup good quality Gruyère cheese, grated
½ cup Parmesan cheese, grated

Preheat oven to 425 degrees.

Quarter fennel bulbs and cut off fronds. Thinly slice fennel about ¼ inch in width.

In a small bowl, blend together cream, salt, and white pepper.

In a medium-sized shallow, ovenproof casserole dish, spread fennel in one layer. Pour cream over fennel. Sprinkle Gruyère over the top. Then sprinkle the Parmesan cheese.

Bake for 20 minutes.

Lower oven to 350 degrees and bake for another 15–20 minutes.

Tip: Can be made a day in advance. Cook for only 20 minutes, then let cool. Cover and refrigerate. Reheat at 350 degrees for 20–25 minutes.

Brussels Sprouts with *Pancetta*

Our traditional Thanksgiving dinner always includes brussels sprouts. They are full of antioxidants and have become much more popular in recent years. Everyone loved this preparation of brussels sprouts, even those who swore they did not care for them. The balsamic vinegar adds sweetness.and the *pancetta* adds a somewhat smoky saltiness. What an extraordinary balance of flavors!

½ pound *pancetta* (Italian bacon), preferably a
    thick slab cut into ¼-inch squares
1 cup chicken broth
4 cups brussels sprouts (wash, trim stems, and
    cut each sprout in half)
½ cup balsamic vinegar

In a large sauté pan, brown the *pancetta*, about 5 minutes. Stir to be sure *pancetta* is browned on both sides. Remove *pancetta* to a small plate.

Add chicken broth and brussels sprouts to pan and bring to a boil. Leave uncovered and lower heat to medium. Cook about 5 minutes until brussels sprouts are al dente. Add balsamic vinegar. Heat for 3 minutes more until vinegar and broth blend and reduce to become a syrup-like liquid. Add *pancetta* and heat for 2 minutes, stirring gently. Serve.

Baked Glazed Yams with Pecans

    6 large yams
    ½ cup shelled pecans, whole for garnish
    1¼ sticks salted butter
    1½ cups dark brown sugar
    1 cup shelled pecans, coarsely chopped

Preheat oven to 350 degrees.

Fill a large pot ¾ full of water. Add yams and boil for about 15 minutes or until yams are tender when pricked with a fork. Drain. Let yams cool for 10 minutes before peeling. Peel skin off each yam. The skin should slip off easily.

Cut yam lengthwise in half and then cut in half crosswise again.

Note: I slice ¼-inch slice off rounded bottom so yam pieces lay flat.

In a large shallow casserole dish, place yams side by side in rows. Place one whole pecan in center of each slice to garnish.

In a small saucepan, melt butter and add brown sugar. Stir until just melted. Pour evenly over yams. Sprinkle yams with chopped pecans.

Bake for about 15–20 minutes.

Spiced Pumpkin Pie with Whipped Cream

Prepare pie dough recipe first. Can be made a day ahead.

Flaky pie dough:

Makes 2 balls for two 9-inch pie pans.

There are many different types of crusts. I prefer to use butter, not shortening. *Pâte Brisée* is a flaky crust with a buttery flavor.

> 2½ cups all-purpose flour
> 2 teaspoons sugar
> ¼ teaspoon salt
> 2 sticks sweet butter, cut into small pieces
> 2 eggs
> 1 tablespoon cold water, plus more if needed

Preheat oven to 350 degrees.

In a medium bowl, add flour, sugar, and salt. In the center of flour, make a well. Add butter and with fingertips blend together until it almost resembles dough. Now add the eggs. Knead again a little with fingertips, then add 1 tablespoon of water. Do not overwork the dough. Blend until it starts to make a ball. If dough is too dry, add an additional 1 tablespoon of water; add a little at a time until the dough sticks together. A food processor makes it easy to prepare the dough, but be careful not to overpulse the dough. Pulsing is key here. Separate dough into two balls and wrap in wax paper. Refrigerate for 45 minutes. Can be refrigerated overnight.

On a lightly floured surface, use a rolling pin to roll out dough until ¼-inch thick. Hold pie plate over the circle of dough and make sure you have at least an inch that will overlap the edge of pie plate. Slowly pick up dough from work surface and put in pie plate.

Cut a piece of parchment paper to fit the bottom of dough in pie plate. Place in center of dough and pour 2 cups of uncooked rice, dried peas, or dried beans on parchment paper to help to hold down the dough and prevent it from shrinking. Place in oven.

Bake for 5 minutes. Remove parchment paper and uncooked rice, dried peas, or dried beans. Cool for 10 minutes. Then pour the pumpkin mixture in and bake as instructed.

Pie filling:

> ½ teaspoon salt
> ¼ cup light brown sugar
> ½ cup sugar
> 1 teaspoon cinnamon
> ¼ teaspoon allspice
> ½ teaspoon ground cloves
> 1¼ teaspoons fresh ginger, finely chopped (if using dried ginger, use ¾ teaspoon)
> 2 eggs
> 2 cups pumpkin purée
> ½ cup half-and-half
> 1 cup heavy cream

Preheat oven to 425 degrees.

Mix first seven ingredients in a bowl. In a separate small bowl, beat eggs, add pumpkin purée, half-and-half, and cream. Add to ingredients in bowl. With a wooden spoon, blend all ingredients together. Pour ingredients in pie shell. Cook for 15 minutes at 425 degrees, then lower to 350 degrees for 40–50 minutes.

Tip: Cover the edges of the primped crust with a strip of tin foil to prevent from overcooking. Pie is done when a toothpick stuck in center comes out clean.

For Whipped Cream recipe, see page 17.

Winter Menus

Holiday Dinner for Six–serves 6
Baby Greens and Dried Cherries with Citrus *Vinaigrette* • *Boeuf Bourguignon* (Traditional French Beef Stew)
Crème Caramel with Grand Marnier

Classic Christmas Day Feast–serves 8 to 10
Elegant Asparagus Soup • Standing Rib Roast with Popovers
Garlic Mashed Potatoes with Chives • String Beans with Dried Cranberries and Shiitake Mushrooms
Profiteroles with Coffee Ice Cream and Dark Chocolate Sauce

Elegant New Year's Eve Dinner for Eight–serves 8
Risotto with *Porcini* and Shiitake Mushrooms • Roast Rack of Veal • Broccoli Purée
Chocolate *Tartufo* Cake

Cozy Dinner for Six–serves 6
Bibb Salad with Maytag Blue Cheese • Veal Stew with Shiitake Mushrooms and Cipollini Onions
Buttered Noodles with Peas • *Sachertorte*

Mid-Winter Family Dinner–serves 4
White Asparagus with Shaved Parmesan Cheese • Rigatoni with Lamb *Ragù* • Cheese Trilogy

Family Get-Together Dinner–serves 4
Lentil and Spinach Soup • Roast Chicken with Allspice and Cinnamon
Bonnie's Baked Mac and Cheese with Cavatappi Pasta • Blueberry Cake with Vanilla Ice Cream

Bistro Dinner for Six–serves 6
Roasted Blue Point Oysters Bistro Style • *Coq au Vin* • *Pappardelle* with Butter
Sautéed Peas and Mushrooms • Mrs. V's Molten Lava Cake Surprise

One-Dish Dinner–serves 4
Orecchiette with Broccoli Rabe and Italian Chicken Sausages
Baked Apples with Vanilla Ice Cream

Sunday Night Dinner–serves 8
Tricolore Salad with Shaved Parmesan • Lasagna with Meat Sauce *Bolognese*
Garlic Bread • *Panna Cotta* with Raspberries and Grand Marnier

Holiday Dinner for Six

serves 6

Baby Greens and Dried Cherries with Citrus *Vinaigrette* • *Boeuf Bourguignon* (Traditional French Beef Stew)
Crème Caramel with Grand Marnier

Boeuf Bourguignon is a traditional French peasant dish originating from the region of Burgundy. Auguste Escofier (known as the Chef of Kings and the King of Chefs) created the most widely known recipe and has turned it into a popular, elegant stew. My adaptation can be an impressive entrée to serve for 6 and also as a buffet dish for 12 or more. It can be made a day ahead. As with most stews, the flavors meld and are better the next day.

Boeuf Bourguignon is traditionally served with potatoes but I prefer buttered noodles with peas (recipe on page 129); always great with any type of stew. If you decide to serve it with potatoes, try the Garlic Mashed Potatoes with Chives (recipe on page 121).

There are a few steps that are important to enhance the flavors of this recipe, so give yourself about an hour for prep time. The rest is cooking time of about 2½ hours. This recipe can doubled to serve 12.

Baby Greens and Dried Cherries with Citrus *Vinaigrette*

Many supermarkets carry organic baby greens, the young, tender mixed lettuce leaves that make it easy to assemble an attractive, colorful salad. Although they are generally prewashed, I always wash was the lettuce prior to using.

During the Christmas season I like to create a festive seasonal salad for an elegant dinner, so I use zesty cherries to decorate the baby greens.

> 5 tablespoons extra virgin olive oil, divided
> ½ cup pine nuts
> 2 navel oranges, plus 4 tablespoons orange juice
> ½ teaspoon sea salt
> 1 16-ounce package organic baby greens
> 1 cup dried red cherries
> Freshly ground black pepper, about 7 grinds or ¼ teaspoon

In a small frying pan, heat 1 tablespoon olive oil. Add pine nuts and stir until golden brown on all sides. Remove from pan as soon as they are done, so that they will not continue browning in the oil. Set aside and let cool.

With a sharp kitchen knife, peel oranges, removing the pith with skin. Over a small bowl, cut out orange sections lengthwise. Save juices. If you do not have enough juice to equal 4 tablespoons, you may need to use the juice from another orange.

In a small bowl, blend orange juice, olive oil, and salt. Put baby greens, pine nuts, and cherries in a large salad bowl. Pour salad dressing over greens and toss with salad tongs. Now add the orange sections and gently toss again. Add pepper and additional salt to taste. Dressing can be made a day in advance, covered, and refrigerated.

Serve immediately.

Boeuf Bourguignon
(Traditional French Beef Stew)

6 ounces salt pork or a 6-ounce piece of thick-slab bacon
3 tablespoons canola or safflower oil
3 tablespoons flour
4 pounds boneless beef for stew, cut into 2-inch pieces (Ask the butcher or meat counter at your grocery store for top shoulder or chuck. Dry beef on a paper towel before dredging in flour.)
15 grinds fresh black pepper
1 teaspoon salt

Vegetables and herbs:

Cheese cloth (optional) and string
½ bunch fresh thyme or ½ teaspoon dried
½ bunch flat parsley with stems, washed
2 bay leaves
3 carrots, peeled and chopped
3 large sweet onions, peeled and chopped
10 peeled garlic cloves, crushed (not chopped; leave whole)
1 bottle full-bodied French Burgundy (such as Pinot Noir)
¾ cup imported Italian plum tomatoes, drained and chopped
2 cups strong beef broth (It might be necessary to use an additional cup of broth or water, making it 3 cups)

Onions and mushrooms:

To be added just prior to serving. Cook separately and add at the end.

18 Cipollini onions
¼ teaspoon sugar
2 tablespoons butter
⅛ teaspoon salt
¾ cup beef broth
½ pound Shiitake mushrooms, wiped clean with a brush or paper towel, stems removed, cap cut in three pieces
½ pound cremini and/or other mushrooms, stems removed, cap cut in half
½ cup red wine

Preheat oven to 325 degrees.

Blanche 6 ounces of salt pork or a 6-ounce piece of thick-slab bacon in 4 cups boiling water for 5 minutes. This removes some of the salt. Remove from water and cut into ½ inch strips about 2 inches long each, called *lardons* in French.

Add oil to a medium-sized ovenproof pot. When hot, sauté strips (*lardons*) of bacon or salt pork for 3–5 minutes until medium brown in color. Remove with a slotted spoon and set aside on a large plate. Retain the bacon drippings in the pot.

In a large Ziploc bag, add flour and beef. Close bag and shake to dredge the beef.

Browning meat:

Turn the heat to medium-high. Bacon drippings and canola should be smoking before you add meat. Add meat in batches. Brown on all sides. Grind some pepper and a large pinch of salt over meat.

Remove meat to a large dish. Discard any burned bits of flour pieces. Add a little more oil if necessary. Repeat until all meat is browned.

While the meat is browning, tie up the herbs in a square of cheesecloth with kitchen string (*bouquet garni*).

Put chopped carrots and onions in the pot once the meat is done and sauté until tender. Add garlic and stir.

Add wine and tomatoes. Add back meat and bacon. Place *bouquet garni* in the center of pot, pushing meat around it.

Add beef broth a cup at a time so it almost covers the meat. Approximately ¾ of the beef should be covered by liquid.

Bring pot to a simmer on low heat on the stove, about 10 minutes.

Cover pot and place in the oven on the middle rack. Cook for about 2 hours. Check meat for tenderness. If meat is not tender, cook for another 30 minutes.

If you are cooking ahead of time, it is best to undercook it slightly.

When the stew is done, remove *bouquet garni*, garlic cloves and bacon pieces with a slotted spoon. Discard.

Remove meat from cooking liquid and strain liquid through a sieve into a large bowl. Press vegetables in sieve to be sure to get all the juices. Return liquid and meat to pot. When ready to serve prepare onions and mushrooms below.

Cipollini onions and mushrooms:

Peel Cipollini onions.

In a medium-sized sauté pan, caramelize onions with sugar, butter, salt, and beef broth. Bring to a boil and cover for 8 minutes. Uncover and stir. Cook until onions are a rich brown color, about 5 more minutes. Add mushrooms. With a wooden spoon, gently blend mushrooms with the onions and the caramelized sauce. Cook for 2–3 minutes more. Remove from heat.

Just before you are ready to serve the stew, add ½ cup of the red wine you will be drinking with the dinner. Heat for another 3 or 4 minutes. Serve.

A fine cabernet sauvignon or any other full-bodied wine is suggested with this dish.

Serve immediately or let cool and refrigerate covered for up to 2 days.

Crème Caramel with Grand Marnier

4 cups 2% milk
1 vanilla bean or 2 teaspoons vanilla extract
8 eggs
1 cup sugar

For caramel:

¾ cup sugar
1 cup water
¼ cup Grand Marnier liqueur

Preheat oven to 350 degrees.

In a medium-sized saucepan, add milk and vanilla. Heat on medium-low heat for 5 minutes. Do not allow it to boil. While milk is heating, beat eggs and sugar together in a large bowl. Slowly fold hot milk into egg mixture.

To make the caramel, put sugar and ½ cup water in a small saucepan. Cook caramel until it turns to a medium amber-brown color. Coat the bottoms of 8 ramekins with caramel about ¼ inch deep. Add ½ cup of water to saucepan with remaining caramel and set aside.

Let ramekins cool for five minutes until caramel hardens.

Now you are ready to add the egg mixture to each ramekin.

If you prefer, you can make the custard in one large soufflé dish instead of the individual ramekins.

Place ramekins in a rectangular roasting pan and fill the pan with water so it reaches halfway up the side of each ramekin.

Bake for 40–50 minutes or until firm. If you use one large soufflé dish, it will take a little longer to cook.

Remove from oven and let cool. Prepare 8 individual dessert plates. Run a butter knife around the circumference of each ramekin. Invert on plate and custard will have the caramel on the top.

Heat the remaining caramel and water. Stir until it becomes liquid again. Add Grand Marnier. Stir for one minute. Spoon sauce over the top of each custard. Garnish with raspberries or strawberries and serve.

Classic Christmas Day Feast

serves 8 to 10

Elegant Asparagus Soup • Standing Rib Roast with Popovers
Garlic Mashed Potatoes with Chives • String Beans with Dried Cranberries and Shiitake Mushrooms
Profiteroles with Coffee Ice Cream and Dark Chocolate Sauce

Christmas has always been my one of my favorite times of year for entertaining. Aside from remembering the spiritual importance of Christmas, which encourages celebration and gathering of family and friends, it is a season filled with magical warmth and reflection. The glow of the fireplace, the tree adorned with lights and our collection of ornaments bring back fond memories of my childhood. For that reason, I always attempt to create a memorable holiday dinner for all attending.

Elegant Asparagus Soup
Serves 10–12

- 4 bunches asparagus
- 2 tablespoons unsalted butter
- 8 large shallots, coarsely chopped
- 3 cups chicken broth
- 2 cups milk
- 1½ cups heavy cream
- ¼ teaspoon freshly grated nutmeg or ground
- Sea salt, to taste
- 1 teaspoon white pepper (freshly ground is preferable)
- 6 tablespoons chives, chopped
- 1 cup *crème fraîche* (optional)

Cut off tough stems from asparagus (the white part). Wash asparagus and place in a large sauté pan filled with an inch or two of water. Water should not cover asparagus. Cook on medium-high heat uncovered, for about 6 minutes or until asparagus spears are just soft and slightly firm.

Drain asparagus and transfer to a plate. To a medium-sized saucepan, add butter and sauté shallots for about 5 minutes until slightly soft, stirring occasionally. Add chicken broth and cook for another 10 minutes.

In a food processor, purée asparagus and chicken broth mixture until creamy and smooth. If lumpy, strain through a medium-sized sieve.

In a medium-sized saucepan, add asparagus mixture, milk, cream, nutmeg, salt, and white pepper. Heat for several minutes on medium-low heat. Taste for added salt and white pepper. Serve in shallow soup bowls. Garnish with chopped chives in center of bowl.

Optional: A dollop of *crème fraîche* in center of bowl.

Standing Rib Roast with Popovers

        4 rib standing rib roast
        1 tablespoon kosher salt
        1 teaspoon black pepper or 20 grinds of fresh
            black pepper
        4 garlic cloves, pressed
        ½ cup red wine
        ½ cup water
        1 cup beef stock
        ½ teaspoon thyme
        ½ teaspoon savory (optional)

Preheat oven to 475 degrees.

Rub roast with salt, pepper, and garlic. In a large roasting pan, place roast with rib side down so that the bones are touching the bottom of pan.

Roast for 15 minutes. Lower heat to 425 degrees and roast for about 1½ hours. Check with a meat thermometer after one hour. When the end of the meat reaches 125 degrees, it will be medium rare on ends. Center should be on the rare side, preferable to most for a rib roast. Keep in mind that you must let the roast stand at least 10 minutes before carving. It will continue to cook as well.

Transfer roast to a large carving board. Remove some of the fat from the roasting pan. Reserve fat for popovers.

For *au Jus*:

Add wine, water, and stock to roasting pan and deglaze. Scrape sides and pieces of brown bits stuck to pan. These brown bits are filled with flavor. Add herbs. Cook for about 3 minutes on top of stove. Strain into a small saucepan. Keep warm on low heat until meat is carved. Place the meat juices in a small decorative pitcher. Pour meat juices over each cut of meat.

Popovers:

  2 tablespoons vegetable oil
  4 cups milk, room temperature
  4 cups sifted flour
  ¼ teaspoon cayenne pepper
  2 teaspoons salt
  6 large eggs

Preheat oven to 350 degrees.

Grease a muffin or popover pan with vegetable oil. Use a pan* with 12 muffin cups (use two pans with 6 cups each if necessary). Heat pan in oven for 10 minutes.

Meanwhile, heat the milk in a small saucepan on medium-low heat for 1 minute to warm and set aside. Sift flour, cayenne pepper, and salt together in a medium-sized bowl.

Slowly stream warm milk into flour and blend. In a small bowl, whisk eggs together before adding to mixture. With a wooden spoon or whisk, blend eggs into flour mixture.

Note: Muffin or popover pan should be very hot before pouring batter into cups.

Fill each muffin cup ⅔ with warm batter and bake for 25 minutes. If necessary, add 5 more minutes until tops are crispy and lightly browned. Remove from oven and serve immediately with lots of butter.

*Popover pans can be purchased at kitchen stores such as Williams-Sonoma

Garlic Mashed Potatoes with Chives

  5 boiling potatoes, peeled
  5 garlic cloves, smashed
  ½ cup milk
  2 tablespoons butter
  2 tablespoons fresh chives, chopped
  Salt and pepper, to taste

Boil water in pot large enough to hold potatoes. Add potatoes and garlic. Boil until potatoes are tender, about 25 minutes. Test by using a fork. Drain water, mash potatoes with a potato masher until lumps are gone.

Add milk and whip. Always add milk slowly so you can see the consistency as you are whipping. Add more milk if needed. The potatoes should not be too loose. I prefer them soft but will still form stiff peaks. Add butter, chives, salt, and pepper to taste. Use a large spoon to give a final whip to the potatoes before serving.

String Beans with Dried Cranberries and Shiitake Mushrooms

  3 tablespoons butter
  ½ cup chicken broth
  ¾ pound string beans
  2 cups Shiitake mushrooms, sliced
  ¾ cup dried cranberries
  Salt and pepper, to taste

Melt butter in a large sauté pan on medium-high heat. Add chicken broth. Bring to a quick boil. Add string beans. Stir. Cook for about 3 minutes. Do not cover.

Add mushrooms and cook for another 3 minutes until string beans are almost done. String beans should maintain their bright green color and should be cooked until slightly soft and al dente. Add dried cranberries. Stir.

Add salt and pepper to taste.

Profiteroles with Coffee Ice Cream and Dark Chocolate Sauce

If you want to make a strong impression on your guests and family, then you will love this classic dessert. Usually served with vanilla ice cream, I added a little twist by filling the *profiteroles* with coffee ice cream. Serve the *profiteroles* with homemade hot chocolate or espresso and your guests will be begging for more!

A favorite among dessert lovers, this classic dessert is most impressive and the *profiteroles* can be made a day ahead. Serve it with homemade hot chocolate sauce and *voila!* An elegant and delicious dessert.

Profiteroles:

If making the *profiteroles* a day in advance, store in a covered airtight plastic or glass storage tray in a dry place.

You will need a food processor or a hand mixer and a wooden spoon to make the pastry dough. Also known as *Pâte à Choux*, a classic dough recipe used to make cream puff pastry.

The dough may be made several days earlier, wrapped in plastic wrap, and stored in the refrigerator.

> 2 cups cold water
> 2 sticks (16 tablespoons) butter
> ¼ teaspoon salt
> 2 cups all-purpose flour
> 8 large eggs
> Large shallow cookie sheet greased with butter or shortening
> Half gallon coffee ice cream

Preheat oven to 400 degrees.

In a medium-sized saucepan, bring water to a boil. Add butter and salt. When butter is melted, remove from heat and add flour. Stir with wooden spoon until mixture leaves the sides and bottom and forms a ball. Remove from pot and let cool for 5 minutes.

In a small bowl, beat eggs with a fork until blended.

In a food processor, add dough and add half of the eggs. Pulse or mix until eggs are blended. Add remaining eggs and mix until blended, about 1 minute.

Lightly butter a large shallow cookie sheet. With a large tablespoon, scoop rounds of dough onto the cookie sheet, leaving 2 inches between each one.

Bake on the middle rack of the oven for 20 minutes. Lower heat to 350 degrees and bake for another 30 minutes or until medium-brown in color. Cool.

With a sharp knife, cut each puff in half horizontally and fill with a small scoop of coffee ice cream. Top with hot chocolate sauce (recipe below).

Garnish with sprigs of fresh mint

Note: The choux pastry puffs can be made a day in advance and stored in one layer on a covered plastic or glass storage tray.

Chocolate sauce:

> 1½ cups milk, divided
> 12 ounces bittersweet chocolate. (A good chocolate with 60% plus cocao is recommended)
> 1 cup sugar
> 2 teaspoons almond extract (optional)

In a saucepan over low heat, add ¾ cup milk and half the chocolate. When chocolate is melted, add the remaining chocolate and sugar. Stir and taste. If necessary, add an additional ¼ cup of sugar. After the ingredients have dissolved, add remaining milk. Add almond extract, if desired. Simmer for 7–10 minutes until sauce is thickened, stirring occasionally.

Can be made ahead and stored for several days. Reheat on low heat. Add an ½ cup more of milk if too thick.

Elegant New Year's Eve Dinner for Eight

serves 8

Risotto with *Porcini* and Shiitake Mushrooms • Roast Rack of Veal • Broccoli Purée
Chocolate *Tartufo* Cake

Rack of Veal is a special, elegant dinner for any season. Veal with the bone in adds flavor to the meat, but boneless is easiest to cut.

Risotto with *Porcini* and Shiitake Mushrooms

½ cup dried *porcini* mushrooms
6–8 cups chicken broth
1½ cups *porcini* liquid
4 tablespoons butter, divided
1 small onion, chopped
2 cups *Risotto* Arborio (Italian rice)
½ cup white wine
½ teaspoon sea salt
Freshly ground pepper, 12 grinds or ¼ teaspoon
     ground pepper
1 packet powdered saffron threads
     or 1 teaspoon saffron threads
8 medium shiitake mushrooms, stems removed
     and tops cut into thirds
1 cup freshly grated Parmigiano Reggiano cheese,
     divided
1 tablespoon flat parsley, chopped for garnish

Dried *Porcini* mushrooms:

In a small bowl add 1½ cups hot water and dried *porcini* mushrooms. Soak for 10 minutes. Using a sheet of paper towel as a strainer, cover another bowl and pour *porcini* mushrooms with liquid through the paper towel. This will strain the liquid and capture the fine dirt and sand found in the mushrooms. Pour the first strained liquid in a large cup or small bowl. The first is the most flavorful and will be used with the chicken broth for the *risotto*.

Add the *porcini* mushrooms one more time to the bowl with a cup of warm water. Wait a few minutes, then strain again with paper towel. Discard this liquid. Cut mushrooms in half.

In a medium-sized saucepan, add chicken broth and reserved porcini liquid. Bring to a boil, then lower heat to keep broth at a simmer.

In a heavy-bottomed saucepan, add 2 tablespoons butter. On medium heat, melt butter, add onion and cook until pearly white, about 3 minutes. Add *risotto* and stir until *risotto* is coated with butter. Now add wine. Stir. Add salt and freshly ground pepper.

Using a soup ladle that measures a ½ cup, scoop one ladle full of broth and add to *risotto*. Stir, when broth is mostly absorbed add another ladle. Repeat for about 17 minutes, stirring every few minutes.

In a small cup, add a ladle of broth and stir in saffron. Mix until blended. When *risotto* is almost done add saffron broth and mushrooms.

When done, *risotto* should be slightly firm. Remove from heat. Add remainder of butter, ½ cup grated cheese, and 2 ladles of broth. Stir. Taste for salt and pepper and serve.

Tip: *Risotto* will continue to cook as you serve it. This is why I like to add an extra ladle or 2 of broth just before serving. Sprinkle with a pinch of chopped parsley on top of *risotto*. Pass extra grated cheese at table.

Roast Rack of Veal

Roast Rack of Veal is an elegant dinner for any season. I generally serve the dish for special occasions. I always serve it with purée of broccoli. The bright green color next to the pink tones of the veal make a beautifully presented main course and is delicous as well.

The veal is best prepared boneless so it is easy to cut. The bone, however, adds much more flavor to the meat as well as keeping it moist. Ask your butcher to remove the meat from the bones and tie it back on the bones. Rule of thumb: 1 bone per person. If the rack has 5 bones it will serve 5–6 persons.

Note: If you purchase the meat at a butcher and the meat is prime quality, cook it at 475 degrees for 40–45 minutes. If you purchase the veal from a supermarket, it is best to cook it at a lower temperature to help tenderize it. Cook it between 400–425 degrees. After searing it on stove, cover it loosely with tin foil for 10 minutes only, then remove.

Veal has a tendency to dry out when overcooked.

> 1 8-pound rack veal
> 2 teaspoons salt
> Freshly ground pepper
> 2 teaspoons dried rosemary or 1 tablespoon
>   coarsely chopped fresh rosemary
> 3 tablespoons olive oil
> 3 tablespoons clarified butter
> 1 pound *pancetta* (Italian bacon)
> 1½ cups dry white wine, divided

Preheat oven to 475 degrees for prime veal or 425 degrees for choice veal.

Salt and pepper the veal. Stick rosemary in meat pockets or creases where string is tied.

Browning veal on stove:

In a medium-sized roasting pan, heat oil and butter on medium-high. When oil and butter are almost smoking, add veal and sear on all sides, about 1–2 minutes on each side. It is very important that the pan is very HOT. You just want to SEAR the meat not cook it. A good way to test the heat is to sprinkle a little water in pan. If it bubbles, it is hot enough. Veal should be browned on both sides.

Remove from heat. Carefully wrap *pancetta* around veal so it covers most of the meat. You may have to lift veal with a kitchen fork to lay *pancetta* slices beneath it. Place in roasting pan so bones are positioned like a rack so meat is not sitting on pan.

Add ¾ cup white wine.

Roast for about 45 minutes. The last 5 minutes turn heat to 500 degrees. Veal is done when the temperature is between 155–160 degrees. Remove from oven. Let rest for 5–10 minutes.

Slice in ¾ inch slices. If juice dries up in bottom of pan, pour in ¼ cup more wine and heat on stove over medium heat. With a wooden spoon, scrape pieces stuck to the bottom of pan. Stir and pour juice through a strainer into a bowl or pouring cup. Pour juices from pan over slices and serve.

Serve with broccoli purée (see recipe on next page). For more color, add a few steamed baby carrots.

Broccoli Purée

2 large bunches broccoli
1 cup water
1 large clove garlic, peeled and cut in half
½ cup chicken broth
6 tablespoons unsalted butter
Salt to taste
¼ teaspoon freshly grated nutmeg or ground
    nutmeg
16 grinds freshly ground white pepper or ½
    teaspoon ground white pepper
2 tablespoons heavy cream

Wash broccoli and cut off bottoms of stalks, leaving most of the upper stalk. There is lots of good sweet flavor in the stalks.

In a medium-sized saucepan, add 1 cup of water, garlic, and broccoli and steam for about 10 minutes. Cover the saucepan, leaving the cover slightly opened. This keeps the broccoli from turning a dark green and overcooking. When broccoli is soft, strain water. Purée broccoli with chicken broth and butter for about 2 minutes or until the broccoli is smooth.

Add salt, nutmeg, and white pepper. If mixture is too thick, add ¼ cup more of chicken broth. Can be done several hours ahead of time.

Stir in heavy cream just before serving. Heat for 2 minutes and serve.

Broccoli purée should have a creamy, yet firm, texture. It should sit on the dish like a scoop of creamy mashed potatoes.

Chocolate *Tartufo* Cake
. . . a Chocolate Lover's Dream

Serves 8–10

For years I have received this special cake as a gift from Fernando Mascia and Gino Mascia, founders of Il Mulino restaurant in New York City and current owners of the top Italian restaurant in Miami Beach, Il Gabbiano. Fernando shared his recipe with me for this ultra rich chocolate cake, which remains my favorite to this day. It is rich, and its pure dark chocolate taste makes your palate hunger for more. It can be made a day in advance. All you need is a bit of whipped cream and you will be serving a most impressive and memorable dessert to your guests.

This cake is very rich. If you cut 2–2½ inch slices, you will be able to serve 10. Secret: It can be frozen for 1 month. You need a 9-inch greased and lightly floured cake pan.

> 24 ounces fine quality dark baking chocolate bars, semi sweet, and preferably 75% cacao. (Fernando uses a Belgian chocolate. There are many fine brands of chocolate available at markets today.)
> ½ cup unsalted butter
> 2 cups milk
> 1 cup sugar
> 1 teaspoon salt
> ¾ cup Grand Mariner liqueur
> 5 eggs, beaten

Preheat oven to 350 degrees.

Break chocolate bars into small pieces. (Do not use chocolate chips.)

If you have a double boiler, fill bottom with water and melt chocolate in top. If you do not have one, in a small saucepan, over medium heat, melt butter and add chocolate, stir until completely melted.

In a medium-sized mixing bowl, add milk, sugar, salt, and Grand Marnier. Stir. Now add melted chocolate. Blend well with a wooden spoon. Add eggs. Mix again until blended.

Grease cake pan with butter and dust with flour on bottom and sides.

Add batter to cake pan.

Important: Place cake pan in a bath of water in a larger pan. Water should come halfway up the side of the cake pan. This helps to prevent the cake from cracking.

Place on middle rack of oven and bake for 1 hour.

Optional: Serve with whipped cream.

Garnish with 3 or 4 red raspberries on each dessert plate.

Cozy Dinner for Six

serves 6

Bibb Salad with Maytag Blue Cheese • Veal Stew with Shiitake Mushrooms and Cipollini Onions
Buttered Noodles with Peas • *Sachertorte*

When the autumn winds start to blow and there's a chill in the air, this veal stew is the perfect dinner. It truly warms the soul.

Sachertorte, as we now know it, was created by a sixteen-year-old apprentice chef, Austrian Franz Sacher, in 1832. It is traditionally served with unsweetened whipped cream. My close friends Donna and Allan Stillman served this delicious version of *Sachertorte* at one of their festive dinner parties. They had spent many winters skiing in Austria and I believe that Donna's version was as good as, if not better than, the one I devoured at the Sacher Hotel in Vienna. Here is my adaptation.

Bibb Salad with Maytag Blue Cheese

- 3 heads bibb lettuce
- 3 tablespoons extra virgin olive oil
- 2 tablespoons aged balsamic vinegar
- ½ teaspoon sugar
- 1 medium red onion, cut into very thin slices
- ¾ cup crumbled Maytag blue cheese
- ½ cup chopped walnuts (optional)
- 3 Bosc pears, washed and cut into ½-inch slices with skin, core removed

Wash and dry bibb lettuce. In a small bowl, add olive oil, balsamic vinegar, and sugar. Blend together with a fork.

In a large salad bowl, add bibb lettuce, onion, and cheese and walnuts. Add dressing and toss lightly. Add pear slices and gently toss again. Serve immediately.

Veal Stew with Shiitake Mushrooms and Cipollini Onions

3 tablespoons olive oil
1½ pounds lean veal
¼ cup all-purpose flour
4 large garlic cloves, chopped finely
1 sweet onion, chopped
½ cup red wine
12 Cipollini onions, peeled
1 bottle beer
1 28-ounce can imported tomatoes
½ pound shiitake mushrooms, cut in half
4 carrots, cut into 1-inch pieces
1 parsnip, peeled and cut into 1-inch pieces
1 teaspoon thyme
1 teaspoon marjoram
1 teaspoon rosemary
1 bay leaf
1 teaspoon salt
1 teaspoon freshly ground pepper
¼ pound string beans, ends trimmed and cut into thirds

Ask the butcher for the leanest veal available for the stew preparation.

Coat a heavy-bottomed stockpot with olive oil. Heat oil over medium-high heat. Lightly coat veal with flour. When oil is very hot, add veal. Brown veal pieces for about 3 minutes, stirring constantly to brown on all sides. Add garlic and stir for one minute, then add chopped sweet onions. Stir for 2 minutes.

Add wine and Cipollini onions. Cook until most of wine is absorbed.

Add beer, tomatoes, mushrooms, carrots, parsnip, and spices.

Bring to a boil. Cover and simmer for one hour. Add the string beans and cook for 30 minutes more. Veal is done when fork tender.

Season with additional salt and pepper to taste.

Serve with parsley buttered egg noodles.

Buttered Noodles with Peas

This classic is usually served with stews. The buttery noodles soak up the robust flavors and make a perfect accompaniment. Also great with meatloaf. A good alternative to mashed potatoes.

1 teaspoon salt
1 pound wide egg noodles (e.g., Pennsylvania Dutch brand)
1½ cups frozen peas
½ stick salted butter, cut into slices
Salt and pepper, to taste
6 sprigs flat parsley, leaves only, chopped finely

Fill a medium-sized pot ¾ with water. Bring to a boil. Add 1 teaspoon salt. Add noodles and cook until al dente, just before done. Noodles are done when noodle is chewy but still slightly firm, not soft. Cook frozen peas according to directions on package. While noodles are cooking, add butter to a bowl. (Optional: Melt butter in a small pot before adding to bowl.)

Drain noodles when done.

Add hot noodles to bowl over the butter. Let sit for one minute to allow butter to melt. Mix with tongs or 2 forks.

Add salt and pepper. Mix.

Sprinkle parsley and mix gently. Serve with peas.

Sachertorte

10-inch round cake pan
12 ounces quality semi-sweet dark chocolate
1¾ cups unsalted butter
12 egg yolks
½ cup confectioners' sugar
½ cup sugar
12 egg whites
¾ cup fine plain breadcrumbs
2 cups apricot jam

Preheat oven to 375 degrees.

Butter the cake pan and sprinkle pan with a small amount of breadcrumbs.

Separate eggs. You'll need two small bowls. Crack each egg and allow egg white to pour out into a bowl. Repeat. Do not let any yolk get into egg whites, otherwise they will not stiffen when mixed. Put yolks in separate bowl.

Place chocolate in a small saucepan on low heat. Using a wooden spoon, stir until melted.

Using either a hand mixer or an electric mixer in a metal or porcelain mixing bowl, cream the butter, egg yolks, confectioners' sugar, sugar, and melted chocolate until it becomes light in color. Clean beaters thoroughly with soap and water and dry with a towel.

In a separate clean bowl, preferably a metal bowl, add egg whites and beat with electric mixer until egg whites are stiff. To test for proper stiffness, use a spoon and dip into the egg whites. It should form soft peaks and egg whites should be shiny. Do not overbeat.

Carefully fold the egg yolk/chocolate mixture into the beaten egg whites by pouring the batter in at the sides first, using a rubber or plastic scraper. Try not to overmix the egg whites and batter. Now gently fold in the breadcrumbs.

Pour mixture into cake pan.

Bake for 1 hour. Turn the oven off after 1 hour and let cake remain in the oven for 10 minutes. Remove from oven. With a sharp knife, lightly go around the sides of the cake before inverting on a plate. Let cake fully cool.

Cut the cake in half horizontally and put top half on another plate. With a flat knife, spread jam on bottom half, then spread jam on top, then place top half, jam side down, on to the bottom half. Spread remainder of jam over the entire cake.

Chocolate glaze:

2⅔ cups confectioners' sugar
½ cup water
8 ounces semi-sweet fine baking chocolate

In a small saucepan, bring confectioners' sugar, water, and chocolate to a boil. Stir while chocolate is melting. Remove from heat and let cool. You can place the pan in a bath of cold water in a larger pot that fits the saucepan to cool. (Fill cold water ½ way up the sides of the saucepan.) After about 10 minutes the chocolate will thicken. Pour the chocolate over top of cake and let drip down sides. Serve with vanilla ice cream or whipped cream.

Cake can be made earlier in the day. Pour glaze on cake just prior to serving.

Mid-Winter Family Dinner

serves 4

White Asparagus with Shaved Parmesan Cheese • Rigatoni with Lamb *Ragù* • Cheese Trilogy

Lamb has always been a favorite of my family. Although most ragùs are usually made with beef, this is a tasty alternative to Italian Beef *Bolognese* Sauce.

White Asparagus with Shaved Parmesan Cheese

1 bunch white asparagus
Salt and pepper
½ cup shaved Parmesan cheese

Preheat oven to 475 degrees.

Wash asparagus and cut off tough end of the stems (usually about ½ inch from bottom).

In a frying pan large enough to hold asparagus in a single layer side by side, add asparagus and fill with water so it reaches halfway up the sides of the asparagus. Cook uncovered for 5 minutes. Do not cook asparagus all the way. Drain water. Add salt and pepper to taste. Be sure stalks are tightly side by side. Lay shavings of Parmesan cheese over asparagus.

Place in top part of oven in pan and bake for 4–5 minutes or until cheese is a light brown. You may have to turn the oven up to 500 degrees. Be sure to use an oven mitt over handle when removing pan from oven. I have had many burned fingers!

Rigatoni with Lamb *Ragù*

3 tablespoons extra virgin olive oil
3 cloves garlic, chopped finely or pressed
3 tablespoons carrots, chopped
3 tablespoons celery (include leaves), chopped
1 small sweet onion or half of large onion, finely chopped
1½ pounds ground lamb (preferably top of leg)
½ cup 2% milk
½ cup red wine
3 cups fresh tomatoes or imported Italian canned tomatoes, chopped
¼ teaspoon fresh ground nutmeg
¼ teaspoon rosemary
1 teaspoon sea salt
12 grinds of fresh black pepper
6 grinds of white pepper or ⅛ teaspoon ground white pepper

Heat oil in a large sauté pan on medium heat. Add garlic and cook for 2 minutes. Add carrots, celery, and onion.

Cook for about 3 minutes until vegetables soften. Add lamb and turn heat up to medium high. Stir and cook until meat is lightly browned, about 4–5 minutes. Add milk and cook for 3 minutes until most of the milk is absorbed.

Add wine and cook until most of wine is absorbed.

Add tomatoes, herbs, salt, and pepper.

Cook lamb *ragù* for 60 minutes uncovered on low. Stir occasionally.

Rigatoni pasta:

1 pound rigatoni pasta
1 teaspoon sea salt
1 cup Pecorino Romano cheese

Cook rigatoni pasta in 8 cups of salted boiling water until al dente. Usually about 10 minutes.

Grate 1 cup Pecorino Romano cheese

Drain pasta and serve with Lamb Ragù with grated Pecorino Romano.

Cheese Trilogy

If you have a specialty market or cheese store in your neighborhood, consider asking them to recommend what cheeses they would suggest for your dessert cheese platter.

6 ounces *Gorgonzola Dolce*
6 ounces Mecox Sunrise cheese from Mecox Bay Dairy, Bridgehampton
6 ounces goat cheese
1 bunch seedless red grapes, snipped into small bunches and washed
2 ripe pears, cored and sliced thinly with skin
1 French baguette, cut in ¾-inch slices

Prepare 4 plates with a wedge of each cheese in the center. Fan half of the pear slices and arrange a small bunch of grapes. Place 4 slices of bread on each plate.

Serve with an Italian dessert wine, like *Vin Santo,* or a glass of port.

Bonnie with Art Ludlow at Mecox Bay Dairy Farm

Family Get-Together Dinner

serves 4

Lentil and Spinach Soup • Roast Chicken with Allspice and Cinnamon
Bonnie's Baked Mac and Cheese with Cavatappi Pasta • Blueberry Cake with Vanilla Ice Cream

When I was growing up, my mother made lentil soup at least twice a month. Lentils are high in fiber, iron, and vitamin B. By adding a little spinach, you have a very healthy and nutritious first course. There were many nights my mother served the soup with flat wide noodles and it became our dinner.

Roast Chicken with Allspice and Cinnamon is a unique preparation. The spices complement the chicken with wonderful, exotic flavors. It has been noted that cinnamon was used as early as 2000 BC and today is used often in different provinces of Lebanon. The fragrant blend of cinnamon and allspice makes this preparation of roast chicken most extraordinary.

Lentil and Spinach Soup

4 cups dried lentils
½ cup olive oil
1 cup onions, chopped
9 cups water
1 teaspoon salt
1 teaspoon ground black pepper
1 pound spinach, cut and washed
2 tablespoons fresh lemon juice
¼ pound *pappardelle* (Italian wide, flat pasta) or wide egg noodles (optional)

Rinse lentils in a colander to be sure there are no stones. In a large pot, heat oil and lightly brown onions. Add lentils, water, salt, and pepper.

Bring to a boil and lower to medium-low heat for one hour. Stir occasionally.

Add spinach and lemon juice (and noodles, if you are using them). Taste for salt and pepper. Cook for 6 minutes.

Remove from heat. Soup should have a medium consistency. If it is too thick, add more water; season again for salt and pepper.

Roast Chicken with Allspice and Cinnamon

1 4-pound organic chicken, quartered
1 tablespoon ground cinnamon
1 teaspoon ground Jamaican allspice
1 teaspoon salt
15 grinds fresh black pepper
Juice of 2 large lemons

Preheat oven to 350 degrees.

Wash chicken parts and pat dry with a paper towel. In a small bowl, mix cinnamon, allspice, salt, and pepper.

Pour lemon juice over chicken. Rub spice mixture all over chicken parts.

Place chicken in a baking pan in one layer. Bake for approximately 60 minutes. If meat is still pink, cook for an additional 10 minutes.

Bonnie's Baked Mac and Cheese with Cavatappi Pasta

I created my version of macaroni and cheese as an alternative to serving my family boxed macaroni and cheese that is full of preservatives. Extra sharp cheddar is a key ingredient and there is nothing better than homemade macaroni and cheese topped with crunchy breadcrumbs.

> 2 8-ounce bars white extra sharp cheddar cheese
> 2 8-ounce bars yellow extra sharp cheddar cheese
> 2½ cups half-and-half
> 1½ teaspoons salt, divided
> ¼ teaspoon black pepper
> ½ teaspoon cayenne pepper
> 24 ounces Cavatappi pasta
> (can substitute a corkscrew pasta)
> 3 tablespoons butter
> ¾ cup plain breadcrumbs (see recipe for freshly made below)

Fresh breadcrumbs:

> 1 loaf day-old bread

In a food processer, coarsely chop a loaf of day-old bread. Crumbs should be small but not powdery. Put breadcrumbs on a flat plate and let dry for 30 minutes. If using fresh bread, you will need to lightly toast them in the oven. See below.

Optional: Bake breadcrumbs in a 450-degree oven for 10 minutes or until breadcrumbs are lightly browned. Let cool and put in an airtight container. Store in a dry place. Can be made a week in advance.

Cheese/cream:

Cut the 4 cheddar cheese bars into 4 pieces each.

In a small saucepan, add half-and-half, cheese, ½ teaspoon salt, pepper, and cayenne pepper.

On low heat, stir mixture until cheese is melted. Remove from heat. Taste for salt. Can be made 2 or 3 hours ahead of serving.

Preheat oven to 425 degrees.

Cavatappi:

Fill a large pot ¾ full with water and bring to a boil. Add 1 teaspoon of salt and pasta. Cook for just a few minutes, al dente. Pasta should be still slightly hard in the center and chewy. If the pasta package directions say cook for 7 minutes, then cook it for 4 minutes and taste. Drain and put pasta back in the same pot. Mix butter into hot pasta so butter is evenly distributed.

If necessary, heat cream and cheese mixture and pour half over cooked Cavatappi and stir to coat pasta evenly. Scoop Cavatappi into a 2½-quart ovenproof casserole dish or individual ramekins approximately 3 inches in diameter and 2 inches deep. Spoon the remainder of the cheese/cream mixture over Cavatappi. (If using ramekins, cream/cheese mixture should fill ¾ of ramekin.)

Sprinkle breadcrumbs on top.

Bake for 10 minutes. Raise oven to 500 degrees and cook for 2 minutes more until breadcrumbs are medium-brown in color.

The key here is not to overcook the macaroni and cheese. It should be moist when served.

Note: Add an additional 5 minutes to cooking time if using one large casserole dish.

Blueberry Cake with Vanilla Ice Cream

Blueberry Cake is simple to prepare and delivers a lovely dessert for any occasion. My dear friend Susan Santefort bakes this often when entertaining at home. Susan, a former Miss Illinois, started entertaining at home for business luncheons and dinners. When visiting me several years ago at my home in Bridgehampton, she brought this blueberry cake wrapped in ribbon.

If you love blueberries, this cake is a must. It's great as a breakfast cake, too.

You will need a greased 9x13 rectangular glass baking dish or pan.

A sifter for flour

> 3 cups cake flour
> 1 teaspoon baking powder
> 1 teaspoon baking soda
> 1 cup sugar
> 1 cup butter
> 2 eggs, beaten
> 1 cup sour cream
> 1 teaspoon vanilla
> 2½ cups fresh blueberries (can use frozen
>   blueberries if fresh are unavailable)

Preheat oven to 350 degrees.

Sift flour into a medium mixing bowl. In this recipe, it is important to sift the flour. If you do not have a sifter, use a sieve and sift with that.

Add baking powder, baking soda, and sugar.

Cut in butter until crumbly. Add eggs, sour cream, and vanilla; beat well. Spread half of batter in the greased baking dish or pan.

Layer blueberries on top of batter; add and spread rest of batter on top.

Topping:

> ¼ cup flour
> 3 tablespoons butter
> ½ cup sugar

Mix together and sprinkle over batter. Bake for 35 minutes.

Can be made a day ahead and covered. No need to refrigerate.

Serve it with vanilla ice cream.

Bistro Dinner for Six

serves 6

Roasted Blue Point Oysters Bistro Style • *Coq au Vin* • *Pappardelle* with Butter
Sautéed Peas and Mushrooms • Mrs. V's Molten Lava Cake Surprise

My special friend from France, Stephane Caporal, the executive chef of Fisher Island Restaurants, Fisher Island, Florida, makes one of the most delicious preparations of *Coq au Vin*. Stephane suggests that it is best made a day or two in advance. It is an excellent selection for a dinner party.

Roasted Blue Point Oysters Bistro Style

24 fresh oysters, opened on the half shell
3 tablespoons salted butter
7 garlic cloves, finely chopped or pressed
Pinch of salt
Pinch of cayenne pepper
¼ cup flat parsley, finely chopped

Preheat oven to 450 degrees.

Opening or shucking oysters is not an easy task. I recommend asking your fishmonger to do it. Oysters, like clams, need to be eaten the same day they are opened. This preparation is similar to escargot, which is a favorite of mine. Why not serve it with oysters! Since many people do not eat raw seafood, roasting the oysters makes this first course safe as well as impressive.

Place oysters on a large cookie sheet or shallow roasting pan.

Melt butter in a small saucepan. Add garlic, salt, and cayenne pepper, and cook for 2 minutes. Remove from heat. Add parsley. Using a tablespoon, spoon mixture over each oyster.

Roast for 3–5 minutes. Butter should be bubbling. Remove from oven and serve immediately. Serve these oysters with crusty French bread.

Coq au Vin

Marinating the chicken in the wine mixture enhances the flavor and tenderizes the chicken. Starting two days ahead and rewarming the dish improves that flavor. This recipe serves 6–8 people, depending on portions.

A day before cooking: Marinate for 24 hours.

Chicken marinade:

   2 bottles French burgundy or California *pinot noir*
   2 large onions, sliced
   4 celery stalks, sliced
   2 large carrots, peeled and sliced
   2 large garlic cloves, peeled and flattened
   2 teaspoons whole black peppercorns
   4 tablespoons olive oil
   2 6-pound roasting chickens, each cut into 8 pieces (2 drumsticks, 2 thighs, 2 wings with top quarter of adjoining breast, 2 breasts)

Cooking chicken:

   2 tablespoons olive oil
   12 ounces thick-cut *pancetta* or *lardons* (salt pork), cut crosswise into strips
   6 tablespoons all-purpose flour
   4 large shallots, chopped
   4 large garlic cloves, chopped
   8 large fresh thyme sprigs
   8 large fresh parsley sprigs
   3 small bay leaves
   4 cups low-sodium chicken broth
   8 tablespoons (1 stick) butter, divided
   2 pounds assorted fresh, wild mushrooms (such as crimini and stemmed shiitake)
   20 1-inch-diameter pearl onions or small boiling onions, peeled
   Fresh parsley, chopped, for garnish

For marinating chicken:

Combine wine, onion, celery, carrot, garlic, and peppercorns in large pot. Bring to boil over high heat. Reduce heat to medium and simmer 5 minutes. Cool completely; mix in oil. Place chicken pieces in large glass bowl. You may need to marinate the chickens in 2 separate bowls.

Pour wine mixture over chicken in bowls, dividing evenly; stir to coat. Cover and refrigerate at least 1 day, turning chicken occasionally.

Note: Can use a large roasting pan for marinating chicken.

For cooking chicken:

Using tongs, transfer chicken pieces from marinade to paper towels to drain; pat dry. Strain marinade; reserve vegetables and liquid separately.

Heat oil in large heavy pot (wide enough to hold chicken in single layer) over medium-high heat.

Add bacon and sauté until crisp and brown. Using slotted spoon, transfer bacon to small bowl.

Add chicken, skin side down, to drippings in pot. Sauté until brown, about 8 minutes per side. Transfer chicken to large bowl.

Add vegetables reserved from marinade to pot. Sauté until brown, about 10 minutes.

Mix in flour; stir 2 minutes. Gradually whisk in reserved marinade liquid. Bring to boil, whisking frequently.

Cook until sauce thickens, whisking occasionally, about 2 minutes. Mix in shallots, garlic, herb sprigs, and bay leaves, then broth. Return chicken to pot, arranging skin side up in single layer.

Bring to simmer; reduce heat to medium-low. Cover pot and simmer chicken 30 minutes. Using tongs, turn chicken over. Cover and simmer until tender, about 15 minutes longer.

Meanwhile, melt 6 tablespoons butter in large heavy skillet over medium heat. Add mushrooms and sauté until tender, about 8 minutes. Transfer mushrooms to a plate. Melt remaining 2 tablespoons of butter in same skillet. Add small onions and sauté until beginning to brown, about 8 minutes. Transfer onions to plate alongside mushrooms; reserve skillet.

Using tongs, transfer chicken to plate. Strain sauce from pot into reserved skillet, pressing on solids in strainer to extract all sauce; discard solids. Bring sauce to simmer, scraping up browned bits. Return sauce to pot.

Add onions to pot and bring to simmer over medium heat. Cover and cook until onions are almost tender, about 8 minutes. Add mushrooms and bacon.

Simmer uncovered until onions are very tender and sauce is slightly reduced, about 12 minutes. Tilt pot and spoon off excess fat from top of sauce.

Season sauce with salt and pepper. Return chicken to sauce. (Can be made 1 day ahead. Cool slightly. Chill uncovered until cold. Cover and keep refrigerated.) Rewarm over low heat.

Remove bay leaves before serving. Arrange chicken on large rimmed platter. Spoon sauce and vegetables over chicken.

Garnish with chopped fresh parsley

Pappardelle with Butter

1 teaspoon salt
16 ounces *pappardelle* (wide flat pasta)
4 tablespoons salted butter, softened
3 tablespoons flat parsley, chopped
½ cup pasta water
Sea salt and pepper, to taste

Bring a large pot of water to boil. Add 1 teaspoon salt. Add *pappardelle* and stir. Cook until al dente. Save a ½ cup of the water, drain the rest of the pasta. Place softened butter in a large bowl. Add drained pasta to bowl and mix until butter is melted. Stir in parsley. If the pasta is dry, add a small amount of the pasta water. Season to taste with salt and pepper.

Sautéed Peas and Mushrooms

1 tablespoon butter
1 tablespoon extra virgin olive oil
2 shallots, coarsely chopped
10 shiitake mushrooms, stems removed and
        mushroom caps cut into ½-inch slices
¼ cup water
2 boxes frozen petite green peas or 1 large bag
        frozen petite green peas (use fresh peas
        when available)
Pinch of salt and black pepper

In a medium-sized sauté pan, heat butter and olive oil. Add shallots. Cook 2 minutes. Stir in mushrooms and cook for 3 minutes.

In a saucepan, bring water to boil. Add peas and stir. Cook until all peas are thawed and slightly hot, about 3 minutes. Drain and add to mushrooms and shallots. This can be done several hours ahead of time. Do not cover until peas are cool. Reheat when ready for 2–3 minutes on stove, add salt and pepper to taste, and serve.

Mrs. V's Molten Lava Cake Surprise

If you are a chocolate lover like I am, you will love this dessert and so will your guests. Stephane gave me the idea for the surprise! *Merci.*

I have added more bittersweet chocolate to the master recipe to satisfy my passion! Chocolate lovers will be in heaven with these molten chocolate cakes.

    1 tablespoon butter for ramekins
    4 ounces (½ cup) semisweet chocolate chips or
        chocolate bar broken in pieces, preferably
        Ghirardelli brand chocolate or any fine
        baking chocolate
    8 ounces (1 cup) bittersweet chocolate 60% or
        more of cacao
    10 tablespoons (1¼ sticks) unsalted butter
    ½ cup all-purpose flour
    1½ cups confectioners' sugar
    3 large eggs
    3 egg yolks
    1 teaspoon vanilla extract
    1 teaspoon coffee liqueur, such as Kahlua
        (optional)
    6 1-inch squares white chocolate

You'll need 6 custard ramekins 4 inches in diameter (6-ounce ramekins) and a baking sheet for ramekins.

Preheat oven to 475 degrees.

Butter bottom and sides of each ramekin.

In a small pot on low heat, melt semisweet and bittersweet chocolate with butter, stirring occasionally. This can also be done in a slightly covered microwaveable bowl for 1½ minutes until soft. Add flour and sugar to the pot or bowl.

Stir in eggs and yolks gradually and stir to blend. Add vanilla extract and stir. Add coffee liqueur, if you desire. Stir. Pour batter into buttered ramekins, filling each ¾ full. Drop a white square of chocolate in the center of each ramekin.

You can prepare up to this point several hours before you are ready to serve them.

In preheated oven, bake cakes for 12–15 minutes. Test for doneness by inserting a toothpick into center of ramekin. Toothpick should be slightly wet. Sides should be firm but center runny. If the toothpick is too wet, cook for another 2–3 minutes.

When done, run a thin, sharp knife around each ramekin and invert each onto a dessert plate.

Serve with either whipped cream or vanilla ice cream. Garnish with 4 or 5 red raspberries by side of cakes.

Serve immediately.

One-Dish Dinner

serves 4

Orecchiette with Broccoli Rabe and Italian Chicken Sausages • Baked Apples with Vanilla Ice Cream

My daughter, Kristin, adores this pasta. She orders it virtually every time she goes to an Italian restaurant and loves it so much that she started cooking it at home. This recipe is Kristin's innovation. It is lighter and has less fat because of the chicken sausage and it's full of flavor. The hot Italian sausage adds a zing to this popular dish.

Many markets today sell fresh-made Italian chicken sausage. If you can't find chicken sausage, use the Italian sweet and hot sausage.

Broccoli rabe (also known as broccoli *di rape*) is Italian broccoli that is important to this dish. It is also high in fiber, slightly bitter, and works well when cooked with garlic and sausage.

Orecchiette with Broccoli Rabe and Italian Chicken Sausages

¼ cup extra virgin olive oil
6–8 large garlic cloves, sliced thinly
1 pound chicken sausage
2 large hot sausages
2 bunches broccoli rabe, thick bottom stems removed. Cut remaining florets and stalks into 3-inch pieces. It is important to use the broccoli florets with part of their stems.
Salt and pepper, to taste
¼ teaspoon crushed red pepper (½ teaspoon if you like it spicy)
2 cups white cannellini beans (precooked). If using canned, rinse before using.

Remove casings from sausage. You may also ask your butcher to remove the casings. Otherwise, cut one end of sausage and squeeze the meat out.

In a large frying pan on medium-high heat add olive oil.

Add garlic and cook for 1 minute. Add sausage and cook for 10 minutes, until lightly browned and cooked through. Add broccoli rabe, salt, pepper, and crushed red pepper. Keep stirring for 5–6 minutes, until broccoli rabe is al dente and still bright green. Gently stir in precooked cannellini beans.

Orecchiette pasta:
small, round, disk-shaped pasta

1 teaspoon salt
1 pound *Orecchiette* pasta
1 cup pasta water

Fill a medium-large pot with water ¾ full. Bring to a boil and add 1 teaspoon salt. Add 1 box (one pound) of *Orecchiette* pasta. Cook for about 8 minutes or until al dente, just before done. Remove 1 cup of pasta water and set aside. Strain pasta in a colander.

Add pasta to the pan with sausage and broccoli rabe and cook over low heat and stir for several minutes until *Orecchiette* is coated with sauce. If pasta is dry, add a little pasta water at a time and mix.

Serve with grated Parmesan cheese on the side.

Baked Apples with Vanilla Ice Cream

4 large apples, such as Gala or Fuji
2 tablespoons unsalted butter, divided
4 tablespoons dark brown sugar, divided
4 scoops vanilla ice cream

Preheat oven to 350 degrees.

Core apples from top only and cut out extra apple flesh to leave a 1½–2-inch round cavity.

Add ½ tablespoon butter and 1 tablespoon dark brown sugar to each cavity.

Place apples in an ovenproof baking pan.

Bake for 20 minutes and baste butter mixture in cavity around top of apple. Bake for another 20–30 minutes until apples are tender and cavity has a brown glaze. Remove from oven and let cool slightly and serve.

Serve with a scoop of vanilla ice cream in cavity of each apple.

Optional: Garnish with a cookie of your choice.

Sunday Night Dinner

serves 8

Tricolore Salad with Shaved Parmesan • Lasagna with Meat Sauce *Bolognese*
Garlic Bread • *Panna Cotta* with Raspberries and Grand Marnier

Salad, lasagna, and garlic bread make a delightful meal for family or friends. This lasagna is made with béchamel sauce and tomatoes and is lighter and full of flavor. Béchamel is commonly used in the preparation for lasagna in Italy.

Lasagna goes well with crusty garlic bread. This is a quick cooking method under the broiler that gives the bread a crispy golden top while remaining soft on the inside.

Tricolore Salad with Shaved Parmesan

This classic Italian salad is a perennial favorite with family and friends. The bitterness of the radicchio adds a nice balance to the endive and arugula. The light green endive, dark green arugula and the red radicchio makes for a dramatic presentation.

    3 large bunches arugula, long stems removed
    1 head radicchio, cut into ½-inch strips
    3 endives, cut into thirds
    16 shavings of Parmigiano Reggiano or ¾ cup
        grated Parmesan cheese

Dressing:

    6 tablespoons extra virgin olive oil
    2 tablespoons red wine vinegar
    ½ teaspoon salt
    ¼ teaspoon fresh ground pepper or 6 grinds
    1 small clove of garlic (or ½ large clove), minced
        or pressed

Wash arugula well. Quickly dip arugula into a bowl of cold water, swishing leaves around for a few seconds to help insure that all sand or dirt is removed.

Wash and cut radicchio and endive. Dry in a spinner or on paper towels. Refrigerate or use immediately.

All lettuce should be chilled and crisp before serving.

Using cheese slicer or sharp thin knife, shave 16 or more shavings of Parmigiano Reggiano cheese.

Mix dressing together in a bottle or bowl. Mix or shake well.

Add greens to salad bowl. Add half of the dressing to salad and mix with salad tongs. Add more dressing, if needed, a little at a time.

Season for salt and pepper.

Serve on salad plates and top each plate with 4 shavings of Parmigiano Reggiano.

Lasagna with Meat Sauce
Bolognese

Lasagna ia a favorite Italian dish that can be made ahead of time. In Italy, most lasagna is made with fresh-made pasta. Instead of mozzarella, many use béchamel sauce. I use fresh pasta because I was told by several Italian chefs that the fresh lasagna is superior to dry lasagna, because it is softer and lighter in texture and absorbs the flavors better. I buy fresh lasagna sheets at Citarella in Bridgehampton or East Hampton, or the Villa Italian Specialties Store in East Hampton.

- ¼ cup olive oil
- 2 carrots, chopped
- 2 stalks celery, chopped
- 1 onion, chopped
- 2 cloves garlic, finely chopped
- 1½ pounds ground beef
- ¾ pound ground pork
- 4 large links Italian hot sausage, casing removed
- 1 teaspoon salt
- ½ teaspoon black pepper
- ¼ teaspoon crushed red pepper
- 1 cup milk
- ¼ teaspoon nutmeg, grated (whole nutmeg can be grated using any grater with smallest grating area)
- 3 28-ounce cans Italian peeled San Marzano tomatoes, preferably certified
- 2 cups ricotta cheese
- 2 teaspoons salt (for water)
- 1 pound lasagna sheets, preferably freshly made lasagna
- 1½ cups béchamel sauce (see recipe at right)
- 1 cup grated Parmesan cheese

Bolognese sauce:

In a stockpot on medium-high, heat olive oil. Add carrots, celery, onion, and garlic. Cook for 2 minutes.

Add meat, salt, pepper, and red pepper. Cook meat until browned, stirring occasionally, about 5 minutes. Add milk and cook until most of milk is absorbed. Add nutmeg and tomatoes and cook for 10 minutes. Stir. Lower heat to a simmer and cook uncovered for 60–90 minutes. Stir occasionally. Add ricotta to sauce and mix. Remove from heat. Taste for salt and pepper.

Preheat oven to 375 degrees.

Béchamel sauce:

- 1 cup milk
- ½ stick butter
- 3 tablespoons flour

In a small saucepan, bring milk to a slow boil. In a medium-sized saucepan, melt butter and add flour, slowly stirring with a wooden spoon until butter and flour become creamy.

Add hot milk slowly, streaming it into mixture (about ¼ cup first). Stir and then add the remainder of milk, stirring briskly. Cook until it becomes thick like cream. Do not cook for more than 2 minutes. Remove from heat. This can be made ahead of time. Add a teaspoon of milk if it becomes too thick when reheating on low heat.

Fill a large pot with water and bring to a boil. Add 2 teaspoons salt. Add lasagna sheets and cook for 3–4 minutes. Remove from pot, put in colander, and rinse with cold water to stop the cooking. Pat dry or shake lasagna sheets to drain water.

Note: If using fresh lasagna, do not precook the noodles.

Butter the bottom of a large rectangular baking dish (10x12). Cover bottom with a layer of lasagna sheets. Spread 3 tablespoons béchamel sauce on sheets. Cover with meat sauce, sprinkle generously with Parmesan cheese. Repeat with another layer of lasagna sheets. Repeat until you have at least four layers. The last layer should be topped with the remaining béchamel, meat sauce, and Parmesan cheese.

Bake in oven for 20 minutes. Serve. (If dry boxed lasagna sheets are used, cook for an additional 15 minutes.)

Garlic Bread

A a garlic bread lover, I am constantly experimenting with new ways to prepare it. Always welcomed among guests, the basket quickly empties whenever I serve it, so I always make extra.

> 5 tablespoons salted butter, softened or melted
> ½ cup extra virgin olive oil
> 8 large cloves garlic, minced or pressed with garlic press
> 1 long loaf Italian bread (semolina or regular)
> 1 teaspoon dried oregano (can be substituted with thyme)

Preheat oven to broil.

In a small bowl, melt butter in a microwave oven for approximately 30 seconds. Be sure to cover bowl with a small plate or a paper towel when microwaving to prevent splattering. Remove from microwave and add olive oil and garlic to butter. Blend.

If you choose to use softened butter, use a fork to press butter into olive oil and garlic.

Cut loaf of bread lengthwise ¾ of way in half, leaving halves attached.

Open halves with your hands and flatten. Spread garlic mixture with a kitchen knife or pastry brush so it covers the inside of both halves. Make sure garlic is spread evenly. Sprinkle with oregano.

Place opened loaf on a rack near top of oven. Watch carefully while bread is in broiler and cook for 1–3 minutes until top is lightly golden and crisp. Do not leave bread while broiling. It can burn quickly under the broiler.

Tip: Broil bread until just lightly golden, then turn oven off and open door. I do this while serving the main course first, followed by a basket of warm bread.

Remove and slice on the diagonal.

Serve in a breadbasket lined with a cloth or linen napkin.

Panna Cotta with Raspberries and Grand Marnier

Serves 8

Panna Cotta (literal translation from Italian is cooked cream) is refreshing Italian custard that has recently become very popular outside of Italy with restaurant chefs and home cooks worldwide. I first tasted this light, flavorful dessert at my friend Dr. Jane Galasso's Water Mill home. It can be served simply plain or topped with a berry mixture. Here is a basic recipe for *Panna Cotta*. It is a perfect, light dessert to serve after a substantial entrée. I top the *Panna Cotta* with raspberries and a splash of Grand Marnier liqueur.

Panna Cotta:

2 tablespoons water
1¼ teaspoons unflavored gelatin
2 cups heavy cream, divided
1¼ cups whole-milk yogurt
1 teaspoon vanilla extract
½ cup granulated sugar
¾ cup–sized ramekins

In a small bowl, add water. Sprinkle unflavored gelatin over water. Let stand for 15 minutes, allowing gelatin to soften.

In a medium-sized mixing bowl, whisk together 1 cup cream, yogurt, and vanilla extract until blended. Set aside.

On medium heat, pour remaining 1 cup of heavy cream into a small saucepan and add sugar. Stir about 1 minute until sugar dissolves. To avoid curdling, do not overheat cream. Remove from heat and add gelatin mixture to hot cream mixture and stir until gelatin is dissolved.

Pour the mixture into the bowl with cream and yogurt. With a wooden spoon, stir until all is blended.

Spoon mixture into each ramekin and refrigerate uncovered until chilled. You can also cover ramekins after they cool, and refrigerate overnight.

Tip: Before inverting ramekin on plate, run a sharp thin knife around the edge to loosen *Panna Cotta* from sides of ramekin. Place plate on top of ramekin, and with one hand on top of the plate and one hand holding ramekin, flip it over so ramekins are inverted onto plate. Tap ramekin lightly with knife or spoon and slowly lift ramekin off.

Raspberries with grand marnier:

2 cups fresh raspberries
½ cup sugar
3 tablespoons Grand Marnier liqueur

In a small bowl, gently toss all ingredients together. Let stand for at least 30 minutes before serving. Can be made several hours before.

Top *Panna Cotta* with raspberry/Grand Marnier mixture and serve.

Note: Ramekins can be purchased at most kitchen stores, such as Williams-Sonoma or online.

Spring Menus

Easter Dinner–serves 6 to 8
Orange and Fennel Salad with Arugula • Leg of Lamb *au Jus* with Vegetables • Greek-Style Potato Wedges
Organic Carrot Cake with Creamy Cream Cheese Frosting

Mezze—Mediterranean Cocktail Party–serves 10
Authentic *Hummus* - Chickpea and *Tahini* Dip • *Kibbeh Nayeh* - a Lebanese-Style Lamb Tartare
Babaganoush - Eggplant and *Tahini* Dip • *Labne* with Dried Mint and Oil - Yogurt Cheese
Spinach and Caramelized Onions • *Lubi B'Zait* - Strings Beans and Tomatoes
Maanek - Lebanese Lamb Sausage Glazed with Lemon and Parsley
Tabouli - Parsley and Cracked Wheat Salad in Romaine Lettuce Boats

Lebanese Buffet Dinner–serves 8 to 10
Fetoush Salad – Lebanese Green Salad • Near-Eastern Spiced Rib Lamb Chops
Koosa – Beirut-Style Stuffed Zucchini with Lamb, Rice, Mint, and Tomato
Eggplant Mediterranean Casserole • Sea Bass with *Tarator* Sauce
Kibbeh Balls • Spinach and Meat Pies • *Kanafe* - Cheese and Shredded Wheat Dessert

An Asian Evening–serves 4 to 6
Chicken Wonton Soup with Bok Choy • Chicken *Soong*
Whole Grilled Red Snapper with Ginger and Scallions • Mary Wang's Simply Delicious Fried Rice
Green Tea Ice Cream

First Grill Night in Spring–serves 6
Penne Pomodoro with Mozzarella • Tuscan Steak with Arugula and Cannellini Bean Salad
Torta di Mele – Tuscan Apple Cake

Spring Is Sprung Dinner–serves 6
Avocado and Crabmeat Salad • Roasted Cornish Hens with Orange Apricot Glaze
Grilled Fresh Asparagus • Wild Rice • Key Lime Pie

Blue Crab Fork-Picking Party for Eight–serves 8
Baby Arugula, Radicchio, and Shrimp Salad • Linguini with Blue Crab Sauce
Vanilla Ice Cream Infused with Fresh Strawberries

From the Peconic Bay–serves 4
Thai Shrimp Soup (*Tom Yaan Goong Nam Con*) • Pan Seared Local Peconic Bay Scallops
Jasmine Rice with Peas • Braised Bok Choy
Grilled Pineapple with Vanilla Ice Cream

Home-Sweet-Home Dinner–serves 4
Gnocchi di Semolina with Tomato Sauce • Roast Chicken Infused with Garlic and Lemon
Sautéed Broccoli • Chocolate Chocolate Brownies

Spring Is in the Air–serves 4
Spinach Salad with Strawberry Yogurt • Wild Salmon with Ginger-Honey Glaze
Quinoa with Vegetables • Berries with *Zabaglione*

Easter Dinner
serves 6 to 8
Orange and Fennel Salad with Arugula • Leg of Lamb *au Jus* with Vegetables • Greek-Style Potato Wedges
Organic Carrot Cake with Creamy Cream Cheese Frosting

Easter is a very special holiday, celebrated in early Spring. Lamb was always the choice in our home for Easter. Occasionally, we would have an Easter ham as well, whenever we had more than 12 people. My mother's delicious recipe for Leg of Lamb *au Jus* is still my favorite preparation. The flavors of the onions, garlic, and herbs permeate the lamb! This is why this lamb preparation needs to be cooked to medium rather than medium rare. What gives this dish an added zing, is my mother's simple trick . . . Lipton's Onion Soup Mix! I often buy lamb and other meats from Catena's in Southampton.

One of my daughter's favorite desserts is carrot cake. The cake is moist and bursting with flavor topped off with irresistible icing. I like to make it with 3 layers. However, two 9-inch pans will work. It serves up to 12 portions, depending on the size of the slice.

Orange and Fennel Salad with Arugula

> 5 large navel oranges
> 2 large bulbs fennel
> 3 bunches arugula
> 8 tablespoons extra virgin olive oil
> 3 tablespoons white wine vinegar
> ½ cup fresh-squeezed orange juice
> Freshly ground pepper and sea salt, to taste

Peel and remove pith and skin from 4 oranges and cut into wedges. Place in large bowl. Cut off green tops of fennel and cut them into 2- by ½-inch strips. Add fennel and arugula to oranges. In a separate bowl, whisk together extra virgin olive oil, vinegar, and juice of one orange. Add pepper and salt to taste.

Leg of Lamb *au Jus* with Vegetables

1 5-pound leg of lamb
3 cloves garlic, peeled and sliced in quarters
3 sprigs fresh rosemary or 1 tablespoon dried rosemary
1 tablespoon salt
1 teaspoon black pepper
1 packet onion soup mix (if it is a large leg of lamb, use 2 packets)
1 cup water
4 baking potatoes, peeled and cut into quarters
4 carrots, peeled and cut on diagonal
Optional: Add small onions to roasting pan with potatoes and carrots.

Preheat oven to 450 degrees.

With a small, sharp knife, cut six ½ inch slices or pockets into the lamb all around the lamb. Stick 2 slices of garlic and a few needles of the rosemary in the pockets. Rub the lamb with salt and pepper. Sprinkle the contents of the dried onion soup packet all over the lamb.

Place lamb in a roasting pan. Pour 1 cup of water in pan.

Cook lamb for 40 minutes. Lower temperature to 375 degrees, add potatoes and carrots (and onions, if using), and cook for 1 hour. If you like the lamb pink, then check for doneness after 1 hour and 15 minutes. Pour ½ cup more water in pan if dry, and stir. When done, remove from oven.

Let stand for 10 minutes. Slice lamb in ¼-inch slices on the bias. Serve on a platter with vegetables around the meat. Pour juices from pan over lamb slices.

Greek-Style Potato Wedges

This is great accompaniment to fish, chicken, lamb, or beef.

4 baking potatoes, preferably Idaho or Russet
3 tablespoons butter
2 tablespoons extra virgin olive oil
Juice of one lemon
2 tablespoons flat parsley, chopped
Salt, to taste

Peel potatoes and cut each potato into 4 wedges. Put potatoes in a bowl of cold water until ready. Can be done 1 hour in advance.

Parboil potato wedges. Fill a large saucepan ¾ full of water. Bring to a boil. Add potato wedges for about 3–4 minutes. Drain.

In a large frying pan, heat butter and olive oil. When bubbling, add potato wedges and brown. Turn wedges over a few times to brown on all sides. Should be slightly crispy and a medium-brown in color.

Remove from heat and sprinkle lemon juice and parsley over wedges. Salt to taste. Serve.

Organic Carrot Cake with Creamy Cream Cheese Frosting

Recipe uses three 9-inch cake pans

  1 teaspoon salt
  2 teaspoons baking soda
  1 tablespoon ground organic cinnamon
  1 teaspoon allspice
  2 cups all-purpose flour
  ¾ cup granulated sugar
  1 cup light brown sugar, firmly packed (can
    substitute dark brown sugar).
  4 large organic eggs
  1 cup safflower oil (can substitute with vegetable
    oil)
  4½ cups organic carrots, shredded (about 11
    medium-large carrots)
  2 teaspoons vanilla extract
  1 cup walnuts, coarsely chopped

Preheat oven to 350 degrees.

In a medium-sized bowl, add salt, baking soda, cinnamon, allspice, flour, granulated sugar, and brown sugar. With a wooden spoon, lightly blend all ingredients. In a large mixing bowl, with a hand-held electric mixer or a stationary electric mixer, add eggs and mix until frothy. Slowly stream in oil. Mix for about a minute. Stir flour mixture into eggs. Add carrots, vanilla, and walnuts. Stir and blend with a wooden spoon.

Spray or lightly butter the bottoms and sides of each cake pan. Line the pans with parchment paper. Butter the top of the parchment paper. Pour in mixture, dividing it evenly among the three pans.

Bake on the middle rack of the oven for 35–40 minutes or until a toothpick placed in the center comes out clean.

Let cakes cool before removing them from pan. Peel off parchment paper and place one cake upside down on a large plate. Ice sides and top. Place another cake upside down on top. Repeat. Now place the third cake upside down and ice on sides and spoon an extra layer on top and give several decorative swirls.

Cream cheese icing:

  2 8-ounce boxes cream cheese
    (preferably Philadelphia brand)
  ½ cup unsalted butter, cut into 1-inch pieces
  2 cups confectioners' sugar
  1 teaspoon vanilla extract

Bring cream cheese and butter to room temperature. With an electric mixer, whip cream cheese and butter until blended. Add confectioners' sugar and vanilla extract. Whip for another several minutes until smooth. Can be refrigerated a day before icing the cake.

Note: It is recommended to prepare the icing and refrigerate for 20 minutes to harden it. This allows for an easier application of icing to the cake.

Mezze—Mediterranean Cocktail Party
serves 10

Authentic *Hummus* - Chickpea and *Tahini* Dip • *Kibbeh Nayeh* - a Lebanese-Style Lamb Tartare
Babaganoush - Eggplant and *Tahini* Dip • *Labne* with Dried Mint and Oil - Yogurt Cheese
Spinach and Caramelized Onions • *Lubi B'Zait* - Strings Beans and Tomatoes
Maanek - Lebanese Lamb Sausage Glazed with Lemon and Parsley
Tabouli - Parsley and Cracked Wheat Salad in Romaine Lettuce Boats

Mezze (pronounced mazza) is popular throughout the Middle East and similar to Spanish tapas. *Mezze* is a mix of numerous small dishes served with drinks.

Mezze is served with lots of pita bread. A very popular dish for *mezze* is raw lamb meat mixed with bulgur wheat. It is called *Kibbeh Nayeh*.

Growing up in our home, *mezze* was served mostly on holidays or before dinner parties. To me, the *mezze* was always more important than the actual dinner! We would devour the *mezze* and often were full by the time dinner was served. This is why *mezze* should be served about two hours before sitting down to dinner.

Authentic *Hummus*
Chickpea and *Tahini* Dip

2 large lemons
½ clove garlic, crushed
1 19-ounce can chickpeas, drained
3–4 tablespoons *tahini*
½ teaspoon salt
2 tablespoons olive oil
½ cup pine nuts

In a food processor, add the juice of 1 lemon, garlic, chickpeas, and 2 tablespoons of *tahini*; process until smooth. Add a tablespoon of water if it is too thick.

The consistency should not be too thick. Add the juice of the second lemon, a little at a time, to taste. Add salt.

My family prefers *hummus* with more lemon flavor. Salt is important also. Add more, if needed.

Pour *hummus* in a shallow serving bowl or small platter with a rim.

Coat the bottom of a small frying pan with olive oil and brown pine nuts. This takes about 2 minutes. Toss them around so they are browned evenly. Pour pine nuts over *hummus* with a little of the olive oil, too. Serve with pita bread.

If you would like to, omit the pine nuts. We also use chopped parsley and add a parsley wreath around the *hummus* on the edge of the bowl or dish.

Kibbeh Nayeh
Lebanese-Style Lamb Tartare

¾ cup bulgur wheat, finely ground (No. 1 grind)
1½ cups warm water
1 cup ice cubes and 1 cup water in a small bowl (used to keep hands cold while kneading meat)
1 pound twice-ground lean lamb meat (from top of leg)
1 large onion, puréed
2 teaspoons salt
1 teaspoon black pepper
½ teaspoon allspice
3 tablespoons extra virgin olive oil
6 scallions, cut into 1-inch pieces
2 medium onions, peeled and cut into ½-inch wedges
4 loaves pita bread, cut into 2-inch triangles

Bulgur wheat:

First soak bulgur wheat. In a medium-sized bowl, add warm water and bulgur wheat and allow to soak for 20 minutes until soft. This finely cut bulgur wheat can be found at most specialty, health food, or Middle Eastern markets.

In another small bowl, add ice cubes and cover with water.

For the lamb:

In a medium-sized bowl, add ground lamb meat. With your knuckles, knead the meat. You must keep your hand cold by sticking it into the ice water every time you knead the meat. Keep folding the lamb meat over while kneading. This should take about 3 minutes.

Now squeeze excess moisture from bulgur wheat in bowl and add ½ cup of wheat to the meat. Mix. Add puréed onion. Add the remainder of bulgur wheat. Dip your hand again in the ice water. Knead again. Add salt, pepper, and allspice. Add more salt and pepper, if necessary. Place *Kibbeh* on a round or oval platter. Mold according to the shape of plate to get a loaflike shape. *Kibbeh* should be 2 inches thick in the center.

Immediately put plate in the freezer for 10 minutes. This will chill the meat and keep it from turning brown in color.

Remove from freezer. With a tablespoon, make 4 half-moon divots on top of meat by sticking the tip of the spoon into the meat about ¼ inch. Drizzle extra virgin olive oil in divots and on top of *Kibbeh*. Garnish with cut scallions and onion wedges around *Kibbeh*. Serve immediately with pita bread.

Babaganoush
Eggplant and *Tahini* Dip

The secret to the best-tasting *babaganoush* is the grilling or broiling of the eggplant. The skin has to be almost burned. The smoky flavor adds a distinctive taste to the eggplant. Serve with pita bread cut into triangles.

   3 large eggplants
   3 large lemons
   2 tablespoons *tahini* (ground sesame with oil)

   1 teaspoon salt
   1 large garlic clove, pressed
   ¼ cup parsley, coarsely chopped

Preheat oven to broil.

Prick each eggplant with a fork in several places. Put eggplants on top rack in oven with a pan beneath it on rack below to catch any eggplant juice.

To get the smoky flavor, char each side of eggplant, turning every 7–10 minutes. Eggplants should be done in between 25–35 minutes. If too much smoke occurs, lower oven to 500 degrees. Watch carefully. Prick eggplant lightly to see if tender before removing from oven. Let eggplant cool slightly.

Squeeze the juice of 2 lemons into a medium-sized bowl. Then peel the dark skin off eggplant and discard along with any dark seeds. The lighter seeds are tender; therefore, you can leave them. Immediately place eggplants in bowl with lemon juice. This stops the eggplant from turning dark in color. Try to get as much of the soft white part of the eggplant covered as possible.

Add *tahini*, salt, and garlic to the eggplant, then taste. Lemon is very important. Add ½ of remaining lemon's juice a little at a time and taste. Whip with a fork until fluffy, about 1 minute. The eggplant will be very soft at this point. Just use a fork and do not purée. You want a few lumps! Garnish with parsley around the edge of bowl.

Labne with Dried Mint and Oil
Yogurt Cheese

   2 cups *labne* (can be bought now at most markets)
   ¼ cup extra virgin olive oil
   ¼ cup dried mint leaves, crumbled

Spoon *labne* into a serving bowl, preferably glass. Stir a little to soften. Add olive oil around and on top of *labne*. Sprinkle generously with dried mint leaves.

Spinach and Carmelized Onions

This is one of my Uncle Jerry's favorite dishes for *mezze*. No matter how busy Jerry Haddad was, flying from city to city with IBM before retirement, he always managed to find time to cook a few favorite dishes, especially on holidays. He prepares it regularly at home to this day.

> 4 medium yellow onions, moon-sliced
> ⅜ cup (approximately 3 ounces) virgin olive oil
> 1 10-ounce package frozen chopped spinach
> 2 tablespoons fresh-squeezed lemon juice
> About ½ cup pomegranate seeds (if available), divided
> ¼ to ½ teaspoon salt
> Pepper, to taste
> ¼ teaspoon sugar, to taste

Use a cast-iron frying pan (if available) to sauté the mooned onions in the oil until they are a deep brown (almost black, but not quite). The onions must be constantly stirred or they will burn and stick to each other and the pan.

Set a fine mesh steel colander over a deep dish to catch the oil, and drain the oil from the onions. Set them aside to drain well and cool.

Steam the frozen spinach until cooked. Let cool until the spinach won't burn your hand. Squeeze the spinach and discard the resulting liquid. Put the spinach in a mixing bowl. Add the lemon juice and toss with a fork or two.

Add about half of the browned onions and about half of the pomegranate seeds (this will leave enough onions and pomegranate seeds to garnish the presentation dish). Add all the oil that has drained from the sautéed onions. Add the salt, pepper, and sugar. Toss well.

Put into the presentation dish and garnish with the reserved onions, then the pomegranate seeds. Serve at room temperature with wedges of pita bread.

Lubi B'Zait
String Beans and Tomatoes

> 1 pound fresh string beans
> ¼ cup extra virgin olive oil
> 2 medium yellow onions, moon-sliced
> 2 medium cloves garlic, finely diced
> 1 10- to 14-ounce can tomato sauce
> ½ teaspoon salt
> 12 grinds fresh pepper

Snip and string the beans and cut into 2-inch lengths; wash and drain.

In a saucepan, add olive oil and sauté the onions until soft. Add the garlic and sauté only a minute longer. Add the tomato sauce, salt, and pepper. Bring to a boil. Quickly turn the heat down to a simmer. Cover and simmer only for thirty minutes. Let cool.

Serve at room temperature or reheat, as desired. Will keep for many weeks if sealed and frozen. If refrigerated, will be good for many days.

Served as a *hors d'oeuvres* (cold) with crackers or pita bread. As side dish for dinner or lunch, it goes very well with rice.

Maanek
Lebanese Lamb Sausage with Lemon and Parsley

Sources: Can buy at Hayat Caterers, Bay Ridge, Brooklyn, NY; Kalustyan, New York City; and some gourmet or Middle Eastern food stores.

> 1 pound *Maanek* (Lebanese lamb sausage)
> Juice of 2 large lemons
> 2 tablespoons chopped parsley

Preheat oven to broil.

Broil sausage links for about 5 minutes, turning them over to brown on all sides. Sausage should be brown but not dry. Remove to a serving plate. Add lemon juice. Stir so all the sausage is coated well. Sprinkle with parsley and serve with pita bread triangles. Sausage is traditionally eaten by dipping a piece of pita bread in the juice first. Next, wrap a sausage link in the bread. Enjoy!

Tabouli
Parsley and Cracked Wheat Salad in
Romaine Lettuce Boats

1 cup fine bulgur wheat
2 cups hot tap water
4 bunches fresh flat parsley, stems removed
14 mint leaves
2 bunches (8) scallions
4 large heads romaine lettuce
4 tablespoons extra virgin olive oil
1 teaspoon salt, divided
¼ teaspoon black pepper
Juice of 3 lemons, divided

In a medium-sized bowl, cover bulgur wheat with hot water and soak for 30 minutes until wheat is soft and most of water is absorbed. Squeeze out any excess water.

Wash and dry parsley, mint, and scallions. Lay on paper towels or spin dry. Parsley needs to be completely dry before cutting.

In a food processor, add parsley, mint leaves, scallions, and 4 large romaine leaves; pulse until chopped. Parsley should be chopped between fine and medium.

Add ¾ cup of bulgur wheat, olive oil, half of the salt, pepper, and juice of 2 lemons. Mix and taste. I always go by taste when making *tabouli*. Salt and lemon juice are important ingredients. It should be on the lemony side. Bulgur wheat tends to absorb salt, so be sure to add more, if needed. Bulgur wheat is an accent to this wonderful salad. Best to add a little less at first. Mix and taste. You can always add more of any ingredient.

Lettuce boats:

The small to medium-sized romaine lettuce leaves make great crispy boats. It is a tradition in our family to eat *tabouli* in romaine lettuce boats when eaten with dinner.

For *mezze*, you can spoon 2 tablespoons of *tabouli* into each leaf and serve on a platter. Or you can serve it in a large bowl in the center of a large plate and surround the bowl with romaine lettuce leaves. Let your guests spoon the *tabouli* into the boats themselves.

I serve *tabouli* also as a first course when entertaining. As the first course, place three lettuce boats on a salad plate. I encourage my guests to pick it up with their fingers or it can be eaten with a knife and fork.

Lebanese Buffet Dinner
serves 8 to 10
Fetoush Salad - Lebanese Green Salad • Near-Eastern Spiced Rib Lamb Chops
Koosa - Beirut-Style Stuffed Zucchini with Lamb, Rice, Mint, and Tomato
Eggplant Mediterranean Casserole • Sea Bass with *Tarator* Sauce
Kibbeh Balls • Spinach and Meat Pies • *Kanafe* - Cheese and Shredded Wheat Dessert

I adore all these dishes. The sea bass preparation is special with the *tahini* sauce (*tarator*). As a matter of fact, when I was a young girl, this was the only way I would eat fish! Sea Bass with *Tarator Sauce* was often served for parties. It is perfect for a buffet, as well as a sit-down dinner. I have used fillets in this recipe; however, it is mostly prepared with a whole fish. The presentation with a whole fish—head and tail—is quite spectacular on the table. You can have your fishmonger clean out the inside. It can be served at room temperature, which is ideal for a buffet.

Kanafe is a popular dessert among Lebanese and Syrian nationalities. *Kanafe* is made with ricotta cheese, and/or a white curd cheese along shredded wheat dough. It is usually served with white simple syrup and, if preferred, rose or orange water. This recipe was passed down to me from my friend Sue Elias. It was passed down to her from my mother's dear, close, family friend, Rose Awad. Her son, Jim Awad, is a dear friend of mine and is often seen on CNN as a financial advisor. I have lots of fond memories of Rose and my mother.

Kanafe has always been a favorite dessert among our friends and family.

Fetoush Salad
Lebanese Style Green Salad

- 2 heads romaine lettuce
- 3 Kirby cucumbers
- 3 ripe tomatoes
- 1 green pepper
- 1 red pepper
- 6 scallions
- 3 radishes
- ½ bunch flat parsley leaves, stems removed
- 8–10 fresh mint leaves, chopped
- 4 tablespoons extra virgin olive oil
- ¼ cup red wine vinegar
- Salt and pepper, to taste
- 3 medium-sized pitas, sliced open, cut into triangles, and toasted until golden

Wash and dry all vegetables. Cut each leaf of the romaine into 3 or 4 pieces. Set aside. Cut off ends of Kirby cucumbers. Cut cucumbers, tomatoes, and peppers into ½-inch cubes. Slice the whites of the scallions and discard ends. Thinly slice the radishes. Coarsely chop parsley and mint. Combine vegetables in a large bowl and add oil, vinegar, salt, and pepper. Crumble pita over salad and toss 15 minutes before serving. This allows the bread to absorb some of the dressing.

Near-Eastern Spiced Rib Lamb Chops

- 2 tablespoons turmeric
- 4 tablespoons allspice (Middle Eastern or Jamaican, preferably)
- 1 tablespoon salt
- ¼ teaspoon cayenne pepper
- 1 teaspoon fresh black pepper
- 16 double-ribbed lamb chops

Preheat your grill or broiler.

Mix all spices together. Ten minutes before you are ready to grill, rub seasoning on both sides of lamb chops just enough to lightly cover sides.

Broil lamb chops for about 7 minutes on one side. Turn over and cook for another 7 minutes. Test for medium rare.

Sear lamb chops on grill for 4 minutes on each side. Total about 8 minutes. Remove from heat. Red meat cooks for several minutes after it's off the grill. Chops are not done at this point. Set aside on a platter and cover when cool. Can be done several hours ahead of time.

When ready to serve, preheat oven to 400 degrees, and reheat for 10 minutes. Check for medium or medium rare.

Koosa
(Beirut-Style Stuffed Zucchini with Lamb, Rice, Mint, and Tomato)

Known as *Koosa* in Beirut, this dish is one of my family's favorites. My friends love them too. In Bridgehampton, I serve this along with grilled spiced rib lamb chops for a spring, summer, or early autumn Saturday night dinner.

Koosa is stuffed zucchini with rice and ground lamb meat cooked in tomatoes with garlic and mint. It can be made with beef. It is served as a dinner entrée or as a side. I use the small zucchinis if I serve them with an entrée.

7 small–medium green zucchini
5 small–medium yellow zucchini
½ cup long grain rice
1 pound ground lamb
½ teaspoon salt
½ teaspoon pepper
2 or 3 lamb bones
1 28-ounce can Italian plum tomatoes
1 cup water
1 tablespoon dried mint
3 whole garlic cloves, smashed (use the flat side of a large knife)

Wash zucchini well. Cut off one end of zucchini. Use a long type of vegetable scooper to take out the pulp from each zucchini. A long carrot peeler will work. Take out as much of the seeds and inside of each zucchini as you can while leaving virtually a shell.

You can use the inside of the zucchini for soups. I love it mixed with butter and eggs for breakfast.

In a medium-sized bowl, mix rice, meat, salt, and pepper, and stuff each zucchini ¾ full. Leave a small space at the top. Rice will expand.

In a large pot, add any bones you have first, then lay zucchini around bottom and layer. Add tomatoes, water, mint, and garlic over stuffed zucchini.

Lay a medium-sized plate over zucchinis. This will keep them from rising while cooking.

Bring to a boil and cover. Turn heat to low. Cook for 50–60 minutes until tender and rice is cooked.

Taste for salt and pepper.

Serve on plate and pour on some of the sauce.

Eggplant Mediterranean Casserole

My dear friend, Nancy Bailey, created this Mediterranean eggplant dish for her holiday parties with family and friends. It is a simpler version than the Lebanese eggplant boats stuffed with lamb and pine nuts that my mother and grandmother use to make. Though this variation is slightly different, it is delicious, and everyone goes back for seconds.

Eggplant:

> 4 medium-sized eggplants

Preheat oven to broil.

Peel and slice eggplants into ½-inch rounds, brush with olive oil, and broil on each side until brown. Remove and set aside.

Lower oven to 350 degrees.

Meat:

> ¼ cup olive oil
> 3 pounds ground lamb
> 3 large onions, cut each in half, then slice into ¼-inch pieces
> ½ cup pine nuts
> 1 tablespoon cinnamon
> 1 tablespoon salt

In a large pan, heat oil and sauté ground lamb. Stir until medium brown. Add sliced onions. Sauté until onion is just transparent. Add pine nuts, cinnamon, and salt and stir. Taste for salt. Add more if necessary.

Tomato sauce:

> 2 15-ounce cans tomato sauce
> 4 cups water
> 2 teaspoons salt
> 1 teaspoon cinnamon
> Optional: 2 tablespoons pomegranate syrup (can be found in specialty or Middle Eastern food markets)

Line eggplant on bottom of serving casserole; add meat, top with rest of eggplant. Make tomato sauce that is equal parts tomato sauce and water. Stir in salt, cinnamon, and pomegranate syrup (if using). Taste for salt and cinnamon. Add more if needed. Pour over casserole and bake until bubbly, about 45 minutes. Add a little more water near the end of cooking if it gets too dry.

Sea Bass with *Tarator* Sauce

Tarator sauce (a *tahini*-based sauce):

> 1 cup *tahini* (ground sesame in olive oil), can be bought at most markets and specialty food markets
> ¾ cup water
> 4 large cloves garlic, minced
> 6 tablespoons lemon juice (about 4 lemons)
> 1 teaspoon sea salt
> Pinch cayenne pepper

In a small bowl, mix all ingredients together. Taste for salt and lemon. *Tarator* should have a lemony flavor. Add more lemon juice, if necessary.

> 3 tablespoons olive oil, divided
> 4 sea bass fillets (can be substituted with yellowtail snapper, red snapper, or any mild white fish). If you prefer a whole fish, ask your seafood monger to clean the whole fish and leave head and tail on.
> ½ teaspoon sea salt
> ¼ teaspoon pepper or 6 grinds freshly ground black pepper
> 1¼ cups water
> 3 large onions, chopped
> ½ cup pine nuts, lightly roasted in olive oil.

Preheat oven to 350 degrees.

Poached fillets:

Brush a large baking pan with olive oil. Lay fillets in baking pan and sprinkle with salt and pepper. Brush fillets with a little more olive oil. Add water to baking pan and poach until just done (don't overcook), about 10–15 minutes depending on the thickness of fillets. Test for doneness with a knife by cutting halfway into a fillet. Fish should be flaky.

Cooking a whole fish:

Sprinkle salt and pepper inside cavity. (Optional: Spread 4 thin slices of lemon inside the cavity. I pick a few sprigs of thyme from my garden and add them to the cavity, too.) Brush skin with olive oil. Add water to pan following directions for poached fillets. Bake for 30-35 minutes or until fish is flaky.

Sauté 2–3 large onions in olive oil until medium-dark brown. In a small frying pan, lightly brown pine nuts with 1 tablespoon olive oil. Stir pine nuts so they do not burn. It takes only 1–2 minutes to lightly brown.

Drain fish on paper towels, place on platter, and cover with *Tarator* sauce.

Sprinkle the onions, then pine nuts on top of sauce.

Kibbeh Balls and Spinach and Meat Pies

I usually purchase these items at Hayat Caterers or Mid East Bakery, both in Bay Ridge, Brooklyn, NY.

Kanafe
Cheese and Shredded Wheat Dessert

Either one 19x12 rectangular roasting pan or two 13x9 baking pans.

Can be frozen without syrup.

> 5 pounds ricotta cheese, drained
> 3 pounds (boxes) Apollo shredded wheat dough (Kataysi and Apollo are popular brands usually found in the frozen section of your grocery store)
> 2 pounds unsalted butter, melted
> ½ cup heavy cream
> ½ cup sugar
> Pinch of salt

Preheat oven to 450 degrees.

Drain ricotta cheese on a paper towel by placing it in a sieve over a bowl for a few minutes and/or squeeze out excess water in ricotta.

Put shredded wheat dough in a food processor; pulse until wheat strands are about ½-inch long. On a large cookie sheet or pan, mix shredded wheat with butter, spreading out the mixture evenly on pan; lightly brown for about 3–5 minutes. Watch it closely so that it does not overbrown. Remove from oven and let cool.

Reduce oven to 400 degrees.

In a large bowl, blend drained ricotta cheese, cream, sugar, and pinch of salt. Stir until there are no lumps.

In roasting pan, add half of shredded wheat (if using two smaller pans, add ¼ of each), spreading it evenly with the palms of your hands. Press shredded wheat gently. Add ricotta mixture and top with remaining shredded wheat.

Bake in oven for 25–30 minutes. Top should be light brown.

Remove from oven and let cool. When ready to use, it is best to serve warm. Cut into 3- or 4-inch squares.

Simple syrup:

> 2 cups sugar
> 1 cup water
> 1 tablespoon lemon juice
> ½ teaspoon rose water (optional)

In a small saucepan, combine sugar, water, and lemon juice. Bring to a boil. Stir until sugar has dissolved. Cook for about 8–10 minutes. Add rose water (if using). Stir and set aside. Let cool. Then refrigerate or serve warm over *Kanafe*.

Drizzle a tablespoon or more syrup on top of each *Kanafe* portion.

Our family dinner on a spring weekend.

An Asian Evening

serves 4 to 6

Chicken Wonton Soup with Bok Choy • Chicken *Soong*
Whole Grilled Red Snapper with Ginger and Scallions • Mary Wang's Simply Delicious Fried Rice
Green Tea Ice Cream

This recipe comes from our dear family friend and chef, who loves to cook with me often for dinner parties. Mary Wang, now an American citizen, was born in Lanchou, China. She has wowed dinner guests with her succulent dumplings and spring rolls.

It is very easy to make fried rice. Mary makes fried rice almost "unfried". She adds the minimal amount of oil. The chicken broth is the key to keeping the rice moist.

Jasmine rice also adds another dimension of flavor to this memorable dish. This fried rice is made with ham but many Chinese Americans today prefer to use ground chicken.

Chicken Wonton Soup with Bok Choy

Mary Wang originally taught me how to make these special wontons. Most supermarkets, today, carry good wonton wrappers. Mary prefers the white wonton wrappers, as do most from the Northeast region in China. In Shanghai, located in the Northeast region, the white wrappers are most popular. They are slightly thicker than the yellow wrappers that are preferred in Southern China.

2 packages white wonton wrappers

For filling:

1½ pounds ground organic chicken (can substitute with ground pork, which is used in most Chinese wontons)
6 stalks scallions, sliced, white and green parts
3 tablespoons fresh ginger, peeled and finely chopped
1 teaspoon salt
15 grinds fresh white pepper (black pepper can substitute)

Vegetables:

3 baby bok choy, cut in half, or 2 large bok choy, quartered
1 small carrot, sliced thinly
4 scallions, sliced thinly, white and light green parts only

Broth:

1½ cups water
1 cup chicken broth (do not use organic stocks because they are too strong)

Paste for sealing wrappers:

2 tablespoons flour, 3 tablespoons water to make a liquid paste to seal wonton wrappers

Mix all filling ingredients in a large bowl.

Lay several wonton wrappers on a board and add 1 teaspoon of chicken filling in center of each wrapper. Dip forefingers into liquid paste and run fingers around edge of wrapper and fold wrapper over, filling in half and then fold both sides in and press (see pictures).

Fill a medium-sized stockpot with water and chicken broth. Bring to a boil. Add wontons and vegetables to boiling broth. Boil for 8 minutes.

In individual serving bowls, add one piece of bok choy, followed by 3 wontons and some of the carrots and scallions. Serve immediately. Freeze the remaining wontons in an Ziploc plastic bag or airtight container.

Chicken *Soong*

2 heads iceberg lettuce, washed and leaves left
    whole
2 tablespoons cornstarch
6 tablespoons water
1½ pounds ground chicken
1 teaspoon salt
2 tablespoons Chinese rice wine
½ tablespoon sugar
6 tablespoons vegetable oil
1 tablespoon garlic, minced
1 tablespoon ginger, minced
½ cup canned water chestnuts, chopped small
½ cup roasted pine nuts
1 tablespoon hoisin sauce
1 cup additional hoisin sauce (for serving)

The key is to leave the whole lettuce leaves intact
by peeling each leaf slowly. Wash and dry. Peel the
remainder of leaves one by one carefully from head
of iceberg. Discard outer tough leaves. The best leaves
are the larger crunchy inner ones.

In a small bowl blend cornstarch and water.

In a medium-sized bowl, add ground chicken, salt,
rice wine, and cornstarch mixture. Mix well. Now add
sugar and blend.

Heat oil in a pan; when it's hot, stir in garlic and ginger
and cook for 2 minutes, then add chicken and stir fry
for 6 minutes.

Add water chestnuts and pine nuts and keep cooking
for 5 more minutes, stirring occasionally. Add 1 tablespoon hoisin sauce.

Taste for salt and pepper.

Serve with a small bowl of hoisin sauce and spoon on
table.

Pass around with a platter of iceberg lettuce leaves.

Explain to your family and guests to take a whole leaf,
spread a teaspoon of hoisin sauce in the middle of the
leaf, and add chicken. Now roll lettuce around center
of chicken mixture. It is a wrap.

Whole Grilled Red Snapper with Ginger and Scallions

    1 3-pound whole red snapper, cleaned and backbone removed
    1 tablespoon fresh ginger, finely chopped
    3 cloves garlic, sliced in thin slivers
    4 scallions (green onions), white part and half of green stem, sliced in ⅛-inch pieces
    1 lemon, thinly sliced in rounds
    3 sprigs thyme
    1 tablespoon peanut oil or extra virgin olive oil

Preheat grill on medium-high heat. For this recipe it is best to have a grill pan for fish.

Rub inside of fish with ginger. Spread garlic slivers and scallions all over the inside of the snapper. Then add lemon slices and 3 sprigs of thyme.

Now rub outside skin with oil on both sides. Spray cooking oil on grill pan. Grill for approximately 7–8 minutes on each side. Turn fish over using 2 large spatulas. Fish should be flaky when done.

Remove to platter. Discard the thyme sprigs and lemon slices inside the cavity before cutting. Drizzle each piece with extra virgin olive oil.

Mary Wang's Simply Delicious Fried Rice

    2 cups uncooked Jasmine rice
    4 cups chicken broth
    4 tablespoons peanut oil (can substitute with vegetable oil), divided
    2 eggs, beaten
    ⅛ teaspoon white pepper
    3 scallions, cut into ¼-inch pieces
    ½ pound small cleaned shrimp (optional)
    ⅓ cup thick-sliced ham, cut into ¼-inch cubes (can substitute organic ground chicken)
    ½ cup green peas
    2 tablespoons fine soy sauce or low-sodium soy sauce

In a medium-sized saucepan over medium-high heat, bring chicken broth to a boil. Add rice and stir for 1 minute. Cover, lower heat to simmer, and cook for 20 minutes. Remove from heat and let stand covered for 5 minutes.

Heat 2 tablespoons oil in a large pan, add the eggs, and fry quickly, scrambling with fork. Add white pepper and cook for a few minutes. Remove eggs from pan onto a plate.

Add 2 more tablespoons of oil to the pan; when hot, add scallions. Stir in shrimp (if using) and ham and stir-fry for 2 minutes.

Now add rice. Stir to mix. Add green peas and eggs. Gently stir and add soy sauce to rice.

Green Tea Ice Cream

    1 pint green tea ice cream

Green tea is often served as a final touch after dinner. After dinner, traditionally, a fruit platter or green tea ice cream is served following a Chinese dinner. In most Chinese families, green tea ice cream is usually served with a red bean sauce. If you are adventurous, you can find the red bean sauce in the Asian section of most supermarkets today.

However, I prefer to offer an assortment of cookies with the green tea ice cream.

Green tea ice cream can be found in the freezer section of most markets. Brands such as Häagen-Dazs make green tea ice cream.

Mary Wang

First Grill Night in Spring

serves 6

Penne Pomodoro with Mozzarella • Tuscan Steak with Arugula and Cannellini Bean Salad

Torta di Mele (Tuscan Apple Cake)

There is nothing better than a sauce made from fresh sun-ripened tomatoes. During the summer months, I go to Pike's Farm Stand in Sagaponack for sweet, ripe, plum tomatoes. In the spring, I buy good quality cans of San Marzano certified tomatoes from Italy. They are among the sweetest tomatoes and make a flavorful sauce.

Make this dinner unforgettable by serving rib eye steaks with the Tuscan salad with cannellini beans cascading off the steak. It is an impressive combination.

The first time I served this steak was with Kevin Penner, pioneer chef of the once-famous Della Femina restaurant, and currently of 1770 House and other East End restaurants. He gave me instruction at my home many years ago while we were hosting a dinner for ten. We had rave reviews from my guests.

Penne Pomodoro with Mozzarella

¼ cup extra virgin olive oil

4 cloves garlic, crushed

4 pounds plum tomatoes or 3 28-ounce cans San Marzano tomatoes

Salt and pepper, to taste

2 tablespoons butter

1½ pounds *penne* pasta

12–24 basil leaves, sliced into thin strips

1 ball freshly made mozzarella, cut into ¼-inch cubes

If using fresh tomatoes, do this step first, then follow recipe. Fill a large pot halfway with water. Add tomatoes and bring to a boil. After about 3 minutes, remove from heat and drain water. Let cool. Peel tomato skins. Skin will peel off easily when cool.

In a sauté pan, heat oil. Add garlic. Cook until garlic is light brown. Pan should be very hot before adding tomatoes. Add tomatoes and stir occasionally, breaking up large chunks. Cook for 15 minutes. Add salt and pepper. Just before serving, stir butter into hot sauce.

Cook *penne* in a pot of boiling water according to directions on the package until *al dente*. Then serve *penne* with sauce and garnish with basil strips and mozzarella cubes.

Tuscan Steak with Arugula and Cannellini Bean Salad

6 rib eye bone-in steaks, cut 1¾ inches thick

Marinade:

- ¼ cup extra virgin olive oil
- 2 garlic cloves, pressed or minced
- 2 teaspoons dried oregano
- 2 teaspoons dried thyme
- 2 sprigs rosemary, chopped
- ¼ teaspoon cayenne pepper
- 2 teaspoons kosher salt or sea salt

Mix ingredients together in a bowl. In a large plate, add steaks and marinade. Make sure steaks are coated well. Refrigerate for 2 hours. Bring steaks to room temperature before cooking.

Cooking methods:

Grill: Steaks can be grilled over high heat for approximately 7–8 minutes on each side for medium rare. Using tongs, rotate steaks away from flare-ups. To test for doneness, press your forefinger on center of steak. Rare steaks will be soft to the touch and medium-rare steaks will be slightly firm.

Grill and Finish in the Oven: I use this method for beef and lamb when entertaining and grill steaks prior to guests arriving or several hours ahead of serving. Grill steaks for about 4 minutes on each side to sear in juices. Steaks will be rare and will have a grilled flavor.

Set aside until ready to serve. Finish them in a 350-degree oven for 10 minutes for medium-rare.

Salad:

- 11 ounces baby arugula (also known as rocket in Italian markets)
- ½ red onion, sliced thinly
- 1 can (drained) or 2 cups cooked cannellini beans

Rinse arugula well. Arugula can be gritty. I fill a small bowl halfway with water, hold the arugula by the stems, and swish it around in the water for about 30 seconds. Either use a spinner to dry or lay arugula on a paper towel for 30 minutes.

Cut off bottom stems where the leaves are very tiny. Add to bowl with sliced onions and cannellini beans. If you are using canned cannellini and they are very starchy, it is best to rinse quickly under cold water. Shake out excess water and add to salad bowl.

Salad dressing:

- 6 tablespoons extra virgin olive oil
- 1 medium garlic clove, pressed or minced
- 4 tablespoons balsamic vinegar
- 1 tablespoon (about 3 sprigs) fresh rosemary, chopped
- Salt and pepper to taste (use fresh-ground black pepper)

Dressing can be done a day ahead, covered and refrigerated.

In a small bowl, mix all ingredients. Whisk until the oil and balsamic vinegar are well blended. Add half of dressing to salad and toss. It is safer to add dressing a little at a time. This will prevent overdressing of the salad. Add more if necessary. Taste for salt and pepper.

Torta di Mele
(Traditional Tuscan Italian Apple Cake)

Torta di Mele is an exceptionally light classic apple cake from Tuscany and very easy to prepare. My childhood friend Patrice Samara shared this recipe with me for this book. Patrice is an Emmy award–winning producer, international stratigist, and writer. She spent a great deal of time in Italy when she was growing up and travels there frequently.

Made with freshly harvested apples in autumn, the *Torta di Mele* can also be just as tasty all year round with the bountiful apples available from your local grocer. The batter does not include butter or lard, nutmeg, cinnamon, allspice, or other ingredients traditionally associated with apple pies or cakes. The shortening used is olive oil and the result is a moist, flavorful cake that is delectable when served warm or at room temperature with espresso or a glass of after-dinner wine. Be prepared to be transported to Italy!

A slice of this versatile cake can also be served at breakfast or with afternoon tea. The *Torta di Mele* has easily become one of our favorite traditional desserts in our family.

> 4 medium apples (golden delicious or granny smith)
> 2 teaspoons fresh lemon juice
> 9 tablespoons flour
> 9 tablespoons sugar
> 6 tablespoons olive oil
> 4 eggs, beaten
> 1 pinch salt
> 1 teaspoon lemon zest (Wash lemon, first. Grate yellow zest only, no pith—white part of peel)
> 1½ teaspoons baking powder

Preheat oven to 350 degrees.

Line a 9- to 10-inch round baking pan with parchment paper, including the bottom and sides of the pan, or butter and lightly flour the bottom and sides of the pan.

Peel, core, and thinly and evenly slice the apples. Pour the lemon juice over the apples and mix. Three of the cut-up apples should be mixed into the batter; the fourth apple will be used for decorating the top of the cake in a circular pattern.

Add flour, sugar, oil, eggs, and pinch of salt to a bowl and mix all ingredients together by hand. Do not over-mix. Add the lemon zest and baking powder. Once everything is well mixed, add the three cut-up apples and continue mixing.

Pour the cake batter into the prepared pan. Tap the batter in the pan to evenly distribute. Decorate the top of the batter with the fourth cut-up apple by pressing the apple pieces into the dough in a circular pattern.

Put the pan in the oven on the middle rack for about 35–45 minutes. Look in the oven at about 35 minutes to check if the cake is cooked by inserting a knife or a toothpick. If it comes out clean, the cake is ready. Otherwise, continue baking another 10 minutes. Check cake again by using a knife or a toothpick. If it comes out clean, the *Torta di Mele* is done.

Serve warm or at room temperature. Can be served with whipped cream or vanilla ice cream.

Spring Is Sprung Dinner

serves 6

Avocado and Crabmeat Salad • Roasted Cornish Hens with Orange Apricot Glaze
Grilled Fresh Asparagus • Wild Rice • Key Lime Pie

This is a recipe that works well with Cornish hens. The sweetness of the apricot and orange with cayenne pepper add zest to these plump birds. I have served this elegant yet economical dish to both family and friends. The presentation of a whole hen on each plate covered with this wonderful glaze is a winner every time. Wild Rice is a classic accompaniment that complements this dish.

I always cherish the months of May and June when asparagus are sold at our local farm stands. They are, to say the least, delectable! There is nothing quite like them when they are just picked. This is a simple yet elegant preparation. It goes with many meat, fish, or poultry dishes.

This sophisticated rice is quite different from white rice in that it has a hard texture and totally different nutty flavor. It takes almost double the time than regular rice to cook. Though it is classically served with duck, wild rice elevates the flavors of the Cornish hen as well.

If you have ever been to Key West, you will find the best key lime pies. There are signs everywhere for the pies. Key lime pie originated in the Keys of Florida where key limes once grew in abundance. They are still grown in sections of the Keys, but after the hurricane in the early 90s many trees were wiped out.

Most pies are traditionally prepared with a graham cracker crust. There are several different versions today, and since my husband prefers a flaky crust as in *Pâte Brisée*, that is what I prepare most often.

Many question why the pie is not lime colored but more yellow. This is due to the citric acid from the key lime's reaction with the yellow egg yolks. If you can find key lmes in a specialty market then you are lucky. Key lime juice is bottled and is used most often in key lime pie. Since fresh is always preferred, I use fresh lime juice in this recipe.

Avocado and Crabmeat Salad

A light and impressive first course. Great for any time of year.

    1 16-ounce can lump crabmeat
    Juice of 3 limes, divided
    2 ripe but firm avocados
    3 tablespoons extra virgin olive oil
    Salt, to taste
    Pinch cayenne pepper (more if you like it a bit
        spicier)

Drain any juice from can of crabmeat. Add juice of 1 lime. Peel avocados and cut into 1-inch chunks. Add to a bowl with juice of 2 limes and olive oil. Gently toss. The lime juice helps to prevent the avocado from turning brown.

Add crabmeat to avocado. Season with salt and cayenne pepper and gently toss.

You may need more lime juice, since some limes are on the dry side. If so, add juice of half a lime first and taste. Add another half if needed.

Serve immediately.

Roasted Cornish Hens with Orange Apricot Glaze

Glaze:

- 2 navel oranges, peels only
- 2 cups water
- ½ cup plus 1 tablespoon orange apricot jam or preserve (brands like Sarabeths carry orange-apricot jam. It can be found in most specialty markets or sections of your supermarket. If you cannot find a blend, buy each separately. Use ¼ cup of each jam and combine.)
- 3 tablespoons granulated sugar
- 2 tablespoons orange liqueur
- ½ teaspoon cayenne pepper

Peel oranges with a small sharp knife to get long strips of peel, if possible.

In a small saucepan, add water and orange peels. Bring to a boil, then lower heat to medium for 20 minutes. Remove orange peels and discard.

Add jam, sugar, orange liqueur, and cayenne pepper to orange liquid in saucepan. Stir and cook 6–8 minutes on low heat until slightly thickened, and it coats a spoon with a light film.

Remove from heat and let cool.

Can be made in advance and stored in the refrigerator in an airtight container indefinitely. Great brushed on ribs and chicken.

Cornish hens:

- 6 Cornish hens
- 1 teaspoon sea salt
- ½ teaspoon freshly ground black pepper
- 3 ½-inch slices orange with skin (placed on side of Cornish hen for garnish—optional)

Preheat oven to 425 degrees.

Wash hens inside and out. Rub cavity with salt and the skin with salt and pepper. Brush each hen generously with ¾ of the glaze.

Bake in oven for 1 hour or until Cornish hens are done. Poultry thermometer should read 180 degrees. On 6 dinner plates, serve one Cornish hen per person. Spoon extra glaze on top of each and garnish with an orange slice, if desired. Any type of rice or potato goes well with these flavorful hens, but wild rice takes it to another level (see recipe on next page).

Grilled Fresh Asparagus

- 2 bunches fresh asparagus
- ¼ cup extra virgin olive oil
- Large pinch of salt
- Freshly ground black pepper

Preheat grill.

Cut off bottom white ends of asparagus. Take a small sharp knife or vegetable peeler and slide it beneath the asparagus's pointed fronds and peel. This step is optional. However it makes for a fancier presentation.

Rub oil on all asparagus. Add salt and lots of freshly ground pepper. Cook on a hot grill for 5–6 minutes, depending on how hot your grill is. Using tongs, turn asparagus after a few minutes when you see grill marks.

Asparagus should be done when slightly soft but still firm.

Wild Rice

1½ cups organic chicken broth
⅓ cup (about 4–5) scallions, finely chopped, white part and light green only
¼ cup pine nuts
½ cup good quality wild rice
Salt, to taste

In a large saucepan, add chicken broth, scallions, and pine nuts. Bring to a boil. Add rice and cover. Adjust heat to simmer for 50–60 minutes. Rice is done when most of broth is absorbed and rice is soft but chewy. If you like the rice harder, drain while there is broth left in pot. Remove from heat and leave covered. Can set aside for up to 30 minutes before serving. Taste for salt.

Stir and serve.

Key Lime Pie

1 *Pâte Brisée* crust (see recipe on page 45); make at least 1 hour ahead.

4 egg yolks
1 can condensed milk
½ cup key lime juice or substitute with fresh lime juice

Note: If using fresh key limes (more tart than regular limes) add 2 tablespoons sugar to recipe.

Preheat oven to 350 degrees.

Roll out dough and place in a pie baking dish or pan. Be sure to leave trim ¼ inch above pan edge for shrinkage. Cut out a piece of parchment paper or wax paper and place in the center of dough in pan. Add 2 cups or a bag of uncooked beans or rice to hold dough down while baking. Bake for 10 minutes.

Filling:

In a bowl, whisk egg yolks for 2 minutes until fluffy. Stir in condensed milk and lime juice (add sugar, if using); mix until thick. Pour filling into prebaked piecrust. Bake in oven for 15–20 minutes. Cool and refrigerate for 1 hour or more before serving. Top with whipped cream before serving. Whipped cream is so easy to prepare that I often whip it up a few minutes prior to serving.

Whipped cream:

1 pint heavy cream
½ cup granulated sugar
½ teaspoon vanilla extract

Can be made several hours ahead of time.

Add cream to a bowl. With an electric mixer, beat until it begins to thicken. Now stream the sugar in while mixing. Add vanilla extract. Continue whipping until cream forms a peak when you stick a spoon in and pull out. Do not overmix. If peaks do not hold for a few seconds, whip for another minute. Cover and refrigerate until ready to use.

Blue Crab Fork-Picking Party for Eight

serves 6

Baby Arugula, Radicchio, and Shrimp Salad • Linguini with Blue Crab Sauce

Vanilla Ice Cream Infused with Fresh Strawberries

The season for blue crabs in the Northeast is from May to September. You can substitute the blue crabs for any other hard-shell crab in your area.

This has been one of the most favorite pastas of mine since I was twelve years old. The flavors of this wonderful sauce are forever imbedded in my memory. I was spending a summer in the Pocono Mountains, when a neighbor with Italian ancestry invited my mother and me over for a dinner of blue crabs and pasta. I know my mother made great pasta, but this topped anything I had ever tasted. The flavor of the blue crabs turned the tomatoes into a spectacular sauce bursting with flavor from the sea.

When I prepare this dish, I go back in time and remember sitting in that tiny kitchen savoring this blue crab pasta with my mother and her friends. I, of course, had seconds. So, if you wish, buy extra crabs and serve them in a separate bowl.

Though messy to eat, it is well worth the effort. Even if you do not opt for picking out the meat from the shells, the pasta stands on it's own, oozing with the crab flavor.

Baby Arugula, Radicchio, and Shrimp Salad

While visiting in Trieste, Italy, I experienced this salad at a restaurant near the port. I love the simplicity and freshness of the arugula with the added punch of tender young shrimp.

> 2 bunches baby arugula or 1-pound container organic baby arugula
> ½ head radicchio leaves, cut into 1-inch slices
> 2 cups water
> 4 peppercorns
> ½ onion, peeled
> 1 pound small shrimp, shelled
> ½ teaspoon salt
> Juice of 1 lemon
> 5 tablespoons extra virgin olive oil
> Salt and pepper, to taste

Wash arugula and radicchio. Spin or air dry on paper towels. Slice radicchio when dry. Refrigerate until ready to use.

Shrimp:

In a medium-sized saucepan, bring water to a boil. Add peppercorns and onion to water. Now add shrimp and salt. Cook for 3–5 minutes until shrimp are tender. Do not overcook.

Drain shrimp and discard onion. Let shrimp cool.

In a salad bowl, mix arugula, shrimp, lemon, and oil. Toss lightly. Season for salt and pepper and serve. You may add a bit more lemon juice, if necessary.

Linguini with Blue Crab Sauce

> 18 fresh live blue crabs (if you prefer to serve 4 crabs per person, 24)

Live crabs:

Fill a large pot that will fit crabs halfway with water and bring to a full boil. Plunge crabs in head first and boil for 2 minutes until crabs are no longer moving. Drain water. Run cold water over the crabs.

To clean:

Open the top shell slightly so you can remove the bitter sac which is filled with dirt. Rinse area to be sure there is no sand. Cut each crab in half with a sharp knife. Set aside.

Tomato sauce:

Can be made a day ahead and refrigerated.

  ¼ cup extra virgin olive oil
  8 cloves garlic, finely chopped or crushed
  2 28-ounce cans Italian imported crushed
     tomatoes (preferably San Marzano tomatoes)
  1 28-ounce can Italian imported whole tomatoes
     (preferably San Marzano tomatoes)
  1 teaspoon dried oregano (if using fresh oregano,
     2 teaspoons chopped oregano)
  ½ teaspoon dried thyme (1 teaspoon freshly
     chopped thyme leaves)
  ½ teaspoon crushed red pepper (¼ teaspoon if
     you like it less spicy)
  1 teaspoon sea salt
  ¼ teaspoon black pepper or 8 grinds freshly
     ground black pepper
  6 sprigs flat parsley, chopped (for garnish)

In a large stockpot heat oil and add garlic. Cook for 2 minutes on medium-high heat. Do not let garlic get brown.

Add tomatoes, oregano, thyme, crushed red pepper, salt, and black pepper. Stir. Cook for 20 minutes, stirring occasionally. This can be done a day ahead.

Add crabs to sauce and cook for another 15 minutes, stirring occasionally.

Taste for salt and pepper

Pasta:

  1 teaspoon salt
  2 boxes (2 pounds) linguini

In a large pasta pot, fill ¾ with water and bring to a boil. Add salt. When ready, add pasta and cook for about 6 minutes or until al dente. Stir occasionally.

When done, strain pasta in a colander. Shake for any excess water. Put pasta back in pot and add enough tomato sauce to coat linguini. Mix lightly with 2 forks.

To serve:

Lobster forks
Pasta bowls or large deep plates

Lobster forks are ideal for picking out the crabmeat. This dish is great served in large pasta bowls or deep flat plates. Of course, you will need extra bowls or plates on the tables for shells.

With a pasta fork, serve each person about 1½ cups pasta. Spoon additional sauce on top of each portion of linguini. Surround each mound with 6 halves of crabs.

Garnish with chopped parsley. Serve immediately.

Vanilla Ice Cream Infused with Fresh Strawberries

Buy one gallon vanilla ice cream. (Or make it homemade if you have an ice cream machine. Follow directions for vanilla ice cream.)

  2 cups fresh strawberries, hulled and cut half
  ¼ teaspoon vanilla
  1 bag frozen strawberries
  ½ cup sugar

Empty ice cream into a medium-sized bowl. Let frozen ice cream soften until you can run a spoon through it. In a small bowl, add fresh strawberries and vanilla. Fold into ice cream. Freeze.

In a small saucepan, heat frozen strawberries and sugar. Stir and cook for 10 minutes on low heat.

Put 2 large scoops of ice cream on dessert plates or in glass bowls. Spoon 2 tablespoons strawberry sauce over ice cream and serve. I often offer chocolate candies or cookies to my guests when serving ice cream.

From the Peconic Bay

serves 4

Thai Shrimp Soup (*Tom Yaan Goong Nam Con*) • Pan Seared Local Peconic Bay Scallops
Jasmine Rice with Peas • Braised Bok Choy • Grilled Pineapple with Vanilla Ice Cream

While traveling through Thailand, I fell in love with a popular soup called *Tom Yaan Goong Nam Con*. I have adapted most of the ingredients, which can be found locally in Southampton and Easthampton as well as in most markets today. Traveling through Thailand was an incredible journey through centuries of religious temples of Buddha towering over the cities and villages. The facades of the temples were decorated in magnificent colors and jewels. The food of Thailand is as colorful as their temples, with a wide spectrum of spices and flavors.

This is a great first course for those who enjoy exotic and spicy flavors. Serve in Asian-style soup bowls—or any soup bowl will do.

Thai Shrimp Soup
(*Tom Yaan Goong Nam Con*)

2 cups chicken broth
2 cups water
6 thin slices ginger, skin removed and finely chopped
4 tablespoons lemongrass, sliced
2 teaspoons sliced red chili
2 shallots, sliced thinly
4 kafir leaves, finely sliced (can be found in freezer sections in most markets)
12 large shrimp, cleaned
4 teaspoons fish sauce
1 tablespoon chili paste (can substitute Thai chili sauce)
4 tablespoons lime juice
1 cup snow peas, cut in half
Pinch sugar
3 sprigs coriander, coarsely chopped

In a medium-sized stockpot, add broth, water, ginger, lemongrass, chili, shallots, kafir leaves, and shrimp. Bring to a boil and simmer. Stir in fish sauce, chili paste, lime juice, and snow peas. Cook for 10 minutes. Taste for seasoning. Add a pinch of sugar.

Cook until shrimp is just done, about 8–10 minutes.

Garnish with fresh coriander leaves.

Pan Seared Local Peconic Bay Scallops

Colin Mather, owner of The Seafood Shop in Wainscott, gets fresh Peconic Bay scallops seasonally. My simple recipe brings out the sweetness of the scallops, and they are irresistible.

    4 tablespoons salted butter
    1 tablespoon canola oil
    ¾ cup all-purpose flour
    ¼ teaspoon sea salt
    ½ teaspoon white or black pepper
    2 pounds Peconic Bay scallops (can substitute
        with any bay scallops)
    2 lemons, cut into wedges

In a large frying pan, on medium high heat, melt butter and add oil. Put flour, salt, and pepper in a Ziploc bag. Dredge the scallops in the bag with flour.

When butter and oil are very hot, add scallops to pan. Cook for 2 minutes on each side. Shake the pan and scallops will flip over or use a slotted spatula to flip them. Scallops should be golden brown and crispy.

Remove scallops to a plate and serve with wedges of lemon.

Jasmine Rice with Peas

Jasmine rice is full of flavor. It goes well with virtually any meat, poultry, or seafood dish. Ideal for an Asian dinner.

    2 cups chicken broth (College Inn or Swanson)
    ½ teaspoon sea salt
    1 cup jasmine rice
    1 box frozen baby peas

In a medium-sized saucepan, bring chicken broth and salt to a boil. When broth is boiling, add rice and stir. Cover and reduce heat to low. Cook for 5 minutes. Now add peas. Stir and cover. Cook for another 15 minutes. Remove from heat. Keep covered and let sit for another 5 minutes. Rice will stay hot for another 20 minutes.

Fluff with a fork and serve.

Braised Bok Choy

4 large bok choy, cut into quarters (if small, serve one per person)
3 tablespoons peanut oil or olive oil
4 garlic cloves, sliced thinly
¼ cup chicken broth
Pinch of sea salt
¼ teaspoon freshly ground pepper

Bok choy is a Chinese cabbage. When sautéed, the flavor is mild and distinctive. It goes well with any meat or fish. It is both unique and impressive served alongside meat or fish.

Clean bok choy well by rinsing under cold water and opening up leaves. This will make sure any dirt is rinsed out. Cut in half lengthwise, then quarter if bok choy is large. Bok choy shrinks in size as it cooks.

In a sauté pan large enough to hold all the bok choy, heat oil. Add garlic slices and cook for 2 minutes on medium heat. Now add bok choy and stir. Add chicken broth, salt, and pepper. Stir every few minutes. Add a bit more broth if it is too dry, but add sparingly. Cook for about 5 minutes. Remove from heat and serve.

Grilled Pineapple with Vanilla Ice Cream

This is a great end to a heavy meal. When grilled, the natural sugars from the pineapple come to the surface. Topped with vanilla ice cream, this simple-to-prepare dessert turns into a special delight.

1 whole ripe pineapple
2 tablespoons safflower oil or canola oil
1 pint vanilla ice cream

Heat grill on high.

Peel and cut pineapple into ¾-inch slices. With a small sharp knife, cut out the core in the center of each slice. This will leave a hole in the middle.

Brush oil on pineapple slices. Place on grill and sear for 2 minutes on one side, then turn over with tongs for another 1–2 minutes. Pineapple should be golden, not burned, with grill marks. Remove and serve with a scoop of vanilla ice cream in the middle of each slice.

Home-Sweet-Home Dinner

serves 4

Gnocchi di Semolina with Tomato Sauce • Roast Chicken Infused with Garlic and Lemon
Sautéed Broccoli • Chocolate Chocolate Brownies

My dear friend Dr. Jane Galasso has prepared this dish often for my family and we are all wild for it. The flavor of the semolina topped with a simple tomato sauce is simply delicious. The unique texture of this style of *gnocchi*, which is a totally different style and shape than the potato *gnocchi* you buy in the store or order in the restaurants, makes for a special appetizer. Great served before a fish or meat course.

Gnocchi di Semolina

4 cups milk
1 cup semolina flour
1½ cup freshly grated *Parmigiano Reggiano*,
    divided
2 teaspoons salt
2 egg yolks, beaten
2 tablespoons melted butter
Pinch of nutmeg

Preheat oven 450 degrees.

In a large saucepan, heat milk until it is almost at a boil. Reduce heat to medium-low. Now add the semolina in a slow stream, mixing as you are pouring. Cook for about 3 minutes. Add ⅔ cup *Parmigiano Reggiano* cheese, salt, egg yolks, butter, and nutmeg. Mix rapidly until well blended. Stir often. The consistency should be similar to thick mashed potatoes. If it is not thick enough, cook for 5 minutes more.

Remove from heat.

Moisten a cutting board with a little water. Do this by sprinkling the water with your hand so there it is not too much water. Spread semolina mixture to ¾-inch thick.

Let cool 30–45 minutes. The dough should not be too moist when ready to cut into circles.

Butter a large baking dish. Use two if necessary.

Use a circle cutter 1½ inches in diameter. You can use a small glass with similar dimensions to cut rounds. Also moisten cutter with water. Cut out circles.

Arrange circles in a row in a single layer, overlapping slightly. Arrange another row overlapping the first row so it looks like a tiled roof (see picture). Repeat until baking dish is filled. Dot with butter and sprinkle a generous amount of Parmesan cheese over the top.

Bake on upper rack of oven for 15 minutes or until golden. If after 15 minutes it has not formed a crust, turn heat up to 500 degrees for 5 more minutes.

Remove from oven and let sit for 5 to 10 minutes before serving.

Remove individual rounds with a spatula. Top with a small amount of tomato sauce. Sprinkle remaining cheese on top and serve.

Gnocchi di Semolina uncooked

Tomato sauce:

    ¼ cup extra virgin olive oil
    1 28-ounce can Italian whole peeled plum
        tomatoes (preferably San Marzano certified)
    1 large whole sweet onion, peeled
    6 tablespoons butter
    1 teaspoon sea salt
    Freshly ground pepper, to taste

In a large saucepan, heat oil on high. When smoking, add tomatoes and whole onion. Cook on medium-high heat for 10 minutes, then simmer for 20 minutes. Use a potato masher to crush tomatoes in saucepan. Add butter, salt, and pepper and stir for one minute. Remove from heat.

The tomato sauce can be made several days ahead and refrigerated.

Roast Chicken Infused with Garlic and Lemon

    1 4–5-pound organic roasting chicken
    1 whole head garlic, top cut off
    4 sprigs fresh thyme or 1 teaspoon dried thyme
    5 lemons

Preheat oven to 450 degrees.

Wash chicken. Pat dry. Rub the outside of chicken with garlic and sprinkle with thyme. Add a few sprigs or a little dried to cavity, too. Add garlic head to cavity. Squeeze the juice of the lemons into the cavity of the chicken. Secure the backside with toothpicks or a small skewer to keep the juice from running out.

In a medium-sized roasting pan, bake chicken for 30 minutes. Then turn heat down to 350 degrees for one hour for a 3½ pound chicken. If 4½–5 pound chicken, cook an additional 30 minutes.

Poultry should be 180 degrees on a cooking thermometer when done.

Sautéed Broccoli

    1 bunch broccoli
    3 tablespoons extra virgin olive oil
    4 garlic cloves, sliced
    ½ cup chicken broth

Wash broccoli and slice into thin florets.

In a medium-sized frying, heat oil. When hot, add garlic slices. On medium-high heat, cook for about 1 minute. Add broccoli florets and sauté for a few minutes. Then drizzle in chicken broth. Stir and heat for about 4 minutes. Add a little more broth if necessary. You do not want the broccoli to be wet.

Chocolate Chocolate Brownies

I love dark chocolate. And with all the talk about the health benefits of chocolate, I wanted to make a chocolate chocolate brownie that had the highest percentage of cacao and was special enough to be served after an elegant dinner. It can be dressed up further with the addition of some raspberries on the side.

1 cup sugar
4 eggs
1 teaspoon vanilla extract
¾ cup flour
1 cup unsweetened premium baking cocoa
½ teaspoon salt
4 ounces premium baking bar bittersweet
    chocolate, 70% cacao
4 ounces semi-sweet premium chocolate baking
    bar, 70%–100% cacao
½ pound (2 sticks) butter
Optional: For dusting, 2 tablespoons
    confectioners' sugar

In this recipe, It is best to use fine quality chocolate bars and break them into pieces. Chocolate chips are not used in this recipe.

In a small bowl, cream sugar and eggs with an electric mixer. Add vanilla extract. Blend until mixture turns a pale yellow, about 2–3 minutes.

In a separate medium-sized bowl, blend flour, cocoa, and salt with a wooden spoon.

Break chocolate bars into small pieces.

In a small saucepan, melt butter slightly, leaving some solid. Reduce heat to low, add chocolate pieces, and allow to melt slowly. Remove from heat and let cool. Stir chocolate into egg mixture and blend well.

Slowly add flour and cocoa mixture, beating with electric mixture for one minute or until blended. Batter can be made several days ahead of time.

Pour into a greased 9- or 10-inch square baking pan. Bake for 25 minutes. Brownie should not be dry.

Test with a wooden toothpick. If it comes out slightly wet, they are done. If still too wet, bake for an additional 5 minutes. Remove and let cool on a rack.

Cut into 3-inch squares. Place a square onto a dessert plate. Dust with confectioners' sugar if you like, and top with a large scoop of vanilla ice cream and/or fruit. Serve.

Spring Is in the Air

serves 4

Spinach Salad with Strawberry Yogurt Dressing • Wild Salmon with Ginger-Honey Glaze
Quinoa with Vegetables • Berries with *Zabaglione*

I love this unique spinach salad and so will your guests. The different textures of the spinach, goat cheese, and walnuts, combined with the strawberry and yogurt flavors, make this a most memorable salad.

Spinach Salad with Strawberry Yogurt Dressing

I prefer to serve this salad in a bowl as opposed to a flat plate. The bowl helps the spinach leaves to stand up. Not only is this salad pleasing to the eye but also to the palate.

Strawberry yogurt dressing:

> 6 large strawberries, hulled
> 2 tablespoons plain yogurt, low fat or regular
> ½ teaspoon sugar (add ¼ teaspoon more if strawberries are not ripe)
> 1 tablespoon extra virgin olive oil
> Pinch of salt

In a food processor or blender, purée all ingredients.

Salad:

> 2 bunches baby spinach
> 4 large strawberries, hulled and sliced thinly
> 16 whole shelled walnuts
> 1 goat cheese log, cut into four ½-inch pieces

Wash spinach and cut off long stems on leaves. Lay on paper towels to dry or spin dry with a salad spinner.

Layer each bowl with bunches of spinach. Add 4 slices of strawberries and the walnuts over the leaves in each bowl. Be sure to place them so they are not all together. Crumble the goat cheese on top of the spinach leaves.

Drizzle each bowl with a full 2 tablespoons of strawberry dressing and serve.

Wild Salmon with Ginger-Honey Glaze

    4 tablespoons amber honey
    2 tablespoons soy sauce
    3 teaspoons fresh ginger, skin removed and finely
        chopped
    2 pounds wild salmon fillets

Preheat oven to 475 degrees.

In a small saucepan, bring the honey, soy sauce, and ginger to a boil for 3 minutes or until glaze is slightly thicker. Stir. Let cool slightly.

Brush glaze on salmon, leaving a little for a final glaze. Roast for 5 minutes. Lower heat to 375 degrees and brush more glaze on salmon fillets. Cook for another 3 minutes. Remove from oven. If fillets are very thin, cut back roasting time by 3 minutes or more. With a sharp thin knife, poke a fillet for doneness. Salmon is best medium rare.

Quinoa with Vegetables

    1 cup quinoa
    1¼ cups water
    ½ red onion, finely chopped
    1 cup mushrooms, sliced in thirds and stems
        removed and discarded
    ½ red pepper, finely chopped
    ¼ green or yellow pepper, finely chopped
    3 sprigs thyme, leaves removed and finely
        chopped, or ½ teaspoon dried thyme
    1 tablespoon extra virgin olive oil
    1 tablespoon balsamic vinegar
    ½ teaspoon sea salt
    ¼ teaspoon freshly ground black pepper
    ⅛ teaspoon cayenne pepper

Rinse quinoa with cold water.

In a medium-sized saucepan, bring water to a boil. Add quinoa and all other ingredients. Cover and lower heat to simmer for 12 minutes. Remove from heat and let rest for 5 minutes. With a fork, fluff quinoa, then serve.

Berries with *Zabaglione*

This dish is great with fresh strawberries, which are available at most farms stands and markets beginning late May. The sweetness of the strawberries are best during the height of their season. You can use just strawberries or feel free to use the mixed berries below.

    ¼ cup sugar
    5 egg yolks
    ½ cup Marsala wine (can substitute sherry,
        Madeira, or white wine)

Mixed berries:

    2 cups strawberries, hulled and cut in half
    2 cups raspberries
    1 cup blueberries

Zabaglione must be cooked by indirect heat. A double boiler is good. If you do not have a double boiler, you can use a metal mixing bowl and large saucepan. Be sure the bowl will fit into the large saucepan.

Fill a large pot ¼ deep with water and bring to a boil, then simmer. If using the double boiler partially fill the bottom pot with water and bring to a boil, then simmer.

With an electric mixer or whisk, cream sugar and egg yolks together in the top pot or mixing bowl until it's pale yellow and has a smooth creamy texture. Can be done an hour ahead of time.

Place bowl or pot with the egg yolks in the larger pot with simmering water and keep whisking. It is best to hold while whisking the pot or bowl so it does not touch the bottom of the pot with water. This is why it is easier to use a double boiler.

Now add the Marsala wine and whisk vigorously. The *Zabagione* will increase in volume as you whisk. Can be served cold, though the classic way is warm.

In 4 to 6 dessert glasses or martini glasses, fill ¾ with mixed berries and top with a heaping tablespoon or two of *Zabaglione*. Serve immediately.

Sources

Art Ludlow's Farm (Turkeys)
855 Mecox Road, Bridgehampton, NY 11932
631.537.0335

Babinski's Farm Stand
160 Newlight Lane, Water Mill, NY 11976
631.726.0194

Briermere Farm (Pies and Farm Stand)
4414 Sound Avenue Riverhead, NY 11901
631.722.3931
briermere.com

Blue Duck Bakery
30 Hampton Road, Southampton, NY 11968
631.204.1701
blueduckbakerycafe.com

Catena's Market (Meat Market and Specialty Foods)
143 Main Street, Southampton, NY 11968
631.283.3456

Citarella's (Bridgehampton and East Hampton)
Montauk Highway, Bridgehampton, NY 11932
631.726.3636
citarella.com

Cromer's Country Market
3500 Noyac Road, Sag Harbor, NY 11963
631.725.9004
cromersmarket.com

Crowleys Farmstand
345 Sagg Main
Sagaponack, NY 11962

Fairview Farm (Harry Ludlow)
19 Horsemill Lane, Bridgehampton, NY 11932
631.537.6154

Green Thumb Organic Farm (Farmer Bill Halsey)
829 Montauk Highway, Water Mill, NY 11976
631.726.1900
greenthumborganicfarm.com

Hayat Caterers, Inc.
(Authentic Lebanese Food and Caterer)
6504 6th Avenue, Brooklyn, NY 11220
718.238.6010
Hyatcaterers.com

Iacono Farm (Chicken Farm)
106 Long Lane, East Hampton, NY 11937
631.324.1107

La Parmigiana Italian Restaurant and Market
(They sell one of the best brands of Italian Imported
San Marzano D.O.P. tomatoes, Strianese)
488 Hampton Road, Southampton, NY 11968
631-283-8030

Kalustyan's Spices and Sweets
(Landmark for fine specialty foods)
123 Lexington Avenue, New York, NY 10016
212.685.3451
kalustyans.com

Mecox Bay Dairy (Art Ludlow)
855 Mecox Road, Bridgehampton, NY 11932
631.537.0335
mecoxbaydairy.com

Mid-East Bakery
(Pita bread made daily, Lebanese cheeses, spices,
sweets)
7808 Third Avenue, Brooklyn, NY 11209
718.680.0561

North Sea Farms
1060 Noyack Road, Southampton, NY 11968
631.283.0735

Pike's Farm
Sagg Main Street, Sagaponack, NY 11962
631.537.5854

Round Swamp Farm
184 Three Mile Harbor Road, East Hampton, NY 11937
631.324.4438

Sant Ambroeus Restaurant
(Gelateria, Pasticceria, Confetteria)
30 Main Street, Southampton, NY 11968
631.283.1233
santambroeus.com

The Seafood Shop
356 Montauk Highway, Wainscott, NY 11975
631.537.0633
theseafoodshop.com

Seven Ponds Orchard
65 Seven Pond Road, Water Mill, NY 11975
631.76.8015

Sources <small>(continued)</small>

Tate's Bake Shop
43 North Sea Road, Southampton, NY 11968
631.283.9830
tatesbakeshop.com

Thomas Falkowski's Farm
Country Garden, Millstone Road, Bridgehampton, NY
11932
631.537.0098

Villa Italian Specialties
7 Railroad Avenue, East Hampton, NY 11937
631.324.5110
villaitalianspecialties.com

Williams-Sonoma
2044 Montauk Highway, Bridgehampton, NY 11932
631.537.3040
williams-sonoma.com

Index